Ex Libris

D1113146

ON THE BOOKS
A Graphic Tale of Working Woes at NYC's Strand Book Store

Greg Farrell

First Printing, November 1, 2014

Published by:
Microcosm Publishing
2752 N Williams Ave
Portland, OR 97227

In the Comix series

For a catalog, write or visit MicrocosmPublishing.com

ISBN 9781621060109

This is Microcosm #160

Distributed in the United States and Canada by Independent Publishers Group and Turnaround in Europe.

Designed by Joe Biel and Meggyn Pomerleau
Edited by Joe Biel
Cover by Greg Farrell

This book was printed on post-consumer paper by union workers in the United States.

"The whole life of the worker is simply a continuous and dismaying succession of terms of serfdom—voluntary from the juridical point of view but compulsory from an economic sense—broken up by momentarily brief interludes of freedom accompanied by starvation; in other words, it is real slavery."

-Mikhail Bakunin c.1869

For the Workers.

I'm sorry I smell.

Greg Farrell

ON THE BOOKS

A Graphic Tale of Working Woes at NYC's Strand Bookstore

Microcosm Publishing
Portland, OR

WHO'S WHO

FRED BASS

Son of Benjamin Bass, Strand's founder. Began working at the store at age 13. Became owner 1956. Currently runs book buying and acquisitions.

NANCY BASS-WYDEN

Co-owner and daughter of Fred Bass. Married to Senator Ron Wyden (D) of Oregon. Began working at the store at age 25.

EDDIE SUTTON

General manager at Strand Books. Oversees day-to-day operations. Worked his way up from clerk. Present at all negotiations.

PABLO VALCARCEL

UAW local 2179 President. Present at the majority of negotiations.

VILMA TORRES-MULHOLLAND

UAW local 2179 Vice President. Present at all negotiations.

AUTHOR'S NOTE:
The comics in this book were written as events took place, mostly over a few months in early summer 2012.

They represent only my personal views and experience, except in the case of the "interstitials," which were sourced from individual workers over roughly the same time span.

Revisions were made for this edition and sections were added in Spring, 2014.

These comics are printed with their original sentiment preserved, though some of my views may have changed since the time of writing.

This book was not commissioned, endorsed, or approved by Strand Books Inc.

...He went into the Strand Bookstore and asked for a book similar to Toni Morrison's *Beloved.*

The young woman behind the counter recommended William Faulkner's

On Amazon, the top results for a similar query lead to another book by Toni Morrison and several books by well-known female authors of color.

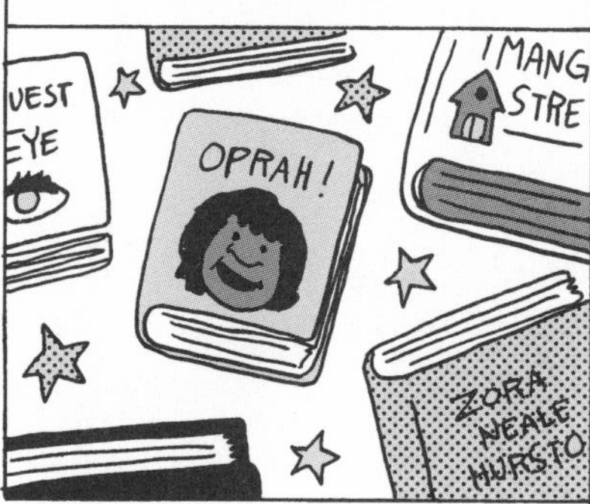

The Strand bookseller made a brilliant, but far-fetched recommendation based more on the character of Morrison's writing

than superficial similarities between Morrison and other authors.

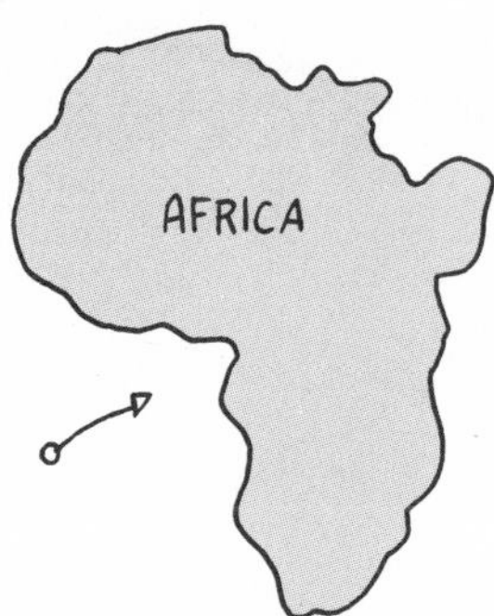

She cut through the chaff of the obvious to make a recommendation that will send the customer home with a new book and returning to the Strand again in the future.

PART ONE

UAW MEMBER

This is to certify that

Greg Farrell

XXX-XX-[redacted]

is a member in good standing in

Local Union 2179, International Union, United Automobile, Aerospace and Agricultural Implement Workers of America (UAW)

Financial Secretary-Treasurer

President

ROADWAY
TH ST
DUTY
STRAND
BOOKSTORE-
A Manhattan institution. Eighteen miles of books and growing. Fiction, history, philosophy—an entire floor of art-related materials, and the famous halfprice review section.
The only thing missing is a coffee shop!
OLD
RARE
NEW
STRAN
BOOKST
$1

Tom Verlaine, Richard Hell, Patti Smith, and countless other New York bohemians (they call us hipsters now) have shuffled these stacks.
Have you seen Tom?!
He's soloing in the break room.

People are drawn to these books because it means more to traffic in books, to be among books, than to sell dental floss in one of the city's numerous pharmacies, for example.
Maybe not to this guy

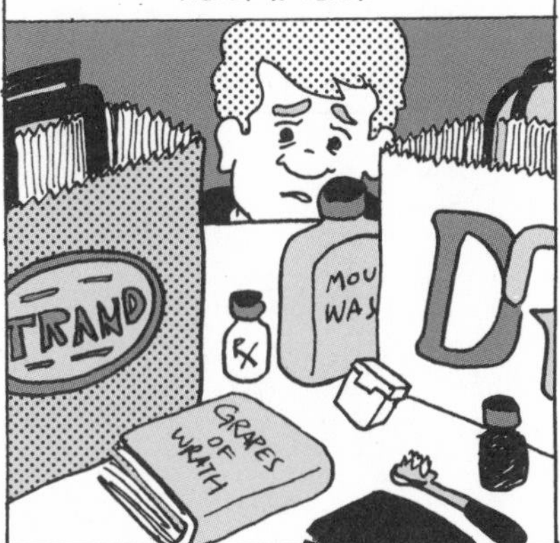
At first, what distinguishes these jobs may not be apparent. Retail is retail.
TRAND
GRAPES OF WRATH
MOU
WAS
RX

Low hourly wages, menial tasks, petty management, and obnoxious customers are all par for course in retail.
$8.00!? Well, then I'll just go on Amazon!
$4.00?! Well, then I'll just go to Wall-greens!

But the Strand is one of a dwindling number of shops in NYC with a unionized work force.

UAW Local 2179: 2,400 members strong, 152 of whom are workers at the Strand Book Store, the Local's largest constituency.

The union protects our rights as workers. It ensures fair wages, benefits, health care, and prevents us from being fired without cause.

The Strand also employs about 30 non-union workers as managers, many of whom have been promoted from within.

Recently, outside hires have been commonplace, as the closure of Borders has left many experienced booksellers unemployed.

This hiring practice has been seen by some as an effort to mitigate the strength of the union and decrease the store's reliance on its members.

I have worked at the store since August 2007. In August 2008, the union contract under which I was hired had reached the end of its previously negotiated three year duration.

A new contract was proposed by the owners, with long-term disadvantages to the workers. One major contention was rising health care contributions increasing at a fixed rate, annually.

Being a relative newcomer and uncertain of my permanence there, I opted for the short term gain and voted yes to the contract (now with $50 signing bonus) despite the urgings of my more experienced colleagues.

The votes were split. A first, according to our union President, and a sign of growing disatisfaction in our ranks.

A revote was taken and the new contract was approved.

Three years later, I'm still here. The Strand is still here. E-readers are here. Borders is gone, along with a sizable portion of Barnes and Noble.

Starting in September 2011, we were without a contract for six months. Negotations were ongoing during that time, with each side making ludicrous demands from the start.
We want one year paid vacation!
We want you to work one year for free.
NEGOTIATE!

However, as time wore on, it became clear that mangagement was serious in their demands.
We're serious. Work a year for free.

In March 2012, Strand extended its "final offer" to the workers: personal days reduced by four, fewer paid holidays, an 18 month wage freeze, and rising health care premiums.
Yo! come to the beach!
I can't. I used my last personal day for Christmas.

Most radical of all: a two-tier structure under which employees hired after the effective date of this contract would receive different, less substantial benefits.
Hired Aug. 31 2011
Hired Sept. 1 2011

A two-tier structure could breed dissent among workers doing the same job for different compensations.
Water...
Water... please
Who wants Jamba Juice!

Tier-two benefits provide little incentive for employees to stay on long-term and will dilute the union as older employees retire or die.
Our "UNION" 2024:
Baby
Hunchback
corporate spy bot

The company has cited a poor economy, the rise of e-readers, and a resulting seven percent decrease in sales since 2009 as reasons for the give-backs.

But there is no evidence to back these claims. Regardless, full time retail salary is not easy to subsist on and allows for little opportunity to save. Why should we take a cut?

Many of us are drawn here from across the country to live in this beautiful, disgusting cutural wasteland. For some, it is our calling.

Many of us come wielding hard-won degrees in art and literature and the load of debt we took on to pay for them.

All of this is what made us attractive hires in the first place. Should we not be compensated for our job-specific knowledge and experience?

Couldn't Duane Reade offer a higher caliber shopping experience if all their employees held degrees in pharmacology?

With Strand's final offer on the table, an informational meeting was held with all Union members and Union officials including President Pablo Valcarcel.

Tensions were high. A growing number of workers are dissatisfied with our union, especially their effectiveness in recent negotiations and their ability to keep constituents informed.

Many felt the union was not acting with our best interest at heart, hoping to put the issue to rest with as little effort on their part as possible.

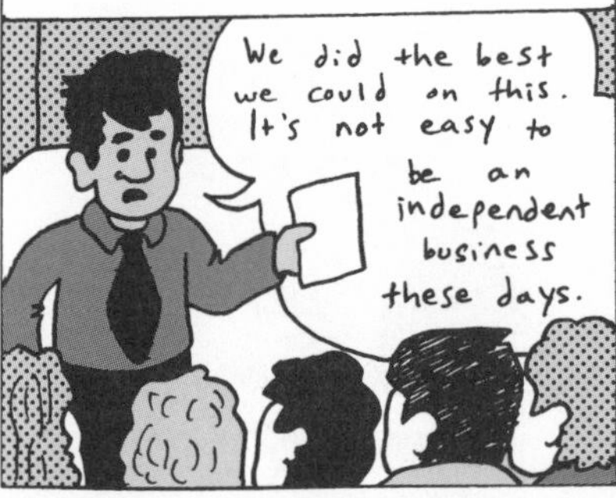

But the people in the room seemed united in their opposition to the terms of the contract.

The following week, the members of UAW local 2175 cast their vote.

On April 5th 2012, it was official. The workers of the Strand Bookstore were overwhelmingly opposed to the terms offered in the new contract and would continue to fight to improve them.

I was hired several years back in the review department.

At the time, the section itself was much bigger and unwieldy. The books were in piles on the floor and on a table where the DVDs are now.

When you got hired in the Review department, you worked in the Review section for months or more until you got your own section.

In the basement, it can get very hot. It was summer. The stated objective—shelve all the books—was unattainable and I was getting paid very little.

What made it worthwhile was the camaraderie, the other weirdos, and of course, the union and benefits at the end of the tunnel.

I used to say, "Welcome to Hell, boys!" in an army voice when I came into work.

I've worked at the Strand for almost one-sixth of my little life.

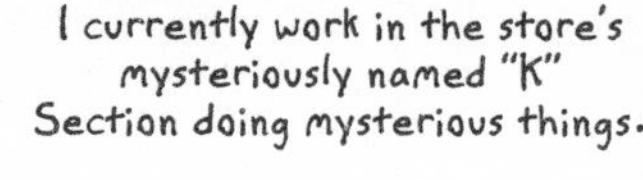

I currently work in the store's mysteriously named "K" Section doing mysterious things.

I'm a born and bred New Yorker. I'm happy to be associated with Strand's slice of New York history, and I'm proud to be unionized.
Whattup QNZ!

I used to work at the Annex until that outpost closed. Total downer. It was very tight-knit and low key. We knew that the main store was busier...

...and we'd heard the employees uptown were snide, self-righteous snobs. But most of us stayed on through the move here to 12th Street.
It was unsettling, though.

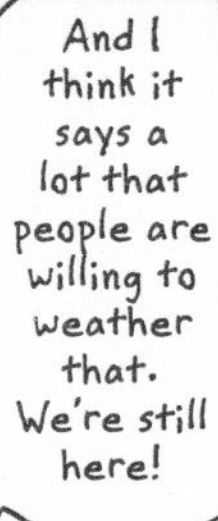

In the five years I've worked here, there have been some major changes and upheavals.
And I think it says a lot that people are willing to weather that. We're still here!

I've been a loyal, diligent employee for five years come August. I feel like I'm well compensated. I live comfortably.

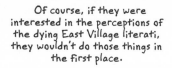

When I moved to New York a year and a half ago, I was hoping to make it big in the literary world...

But it turns out unpaid internships are not a sustainable life choice. With Strand, I could pay my bills while doing what I love—sharing words with others.
As a writer or bookseller.

When I realized ownership was trying to turn the store into a corporate parody of itself by pushing a union busting contract...

I knew I had to do whatever I could to preserve the wonderful, dusty community bookstore that enticed me to the city when I first visited as a teenager.

I also discovered a wonderful community of coworkers and friends who would fight to preserve it with me.

Trying to make it in the lit world by sitting at home sending out cover letters is nowhere near as fulfilling as joining together to defend our common dreams.

Strand workers are unionized by Local 2179 of THE UNITED AUTO WORKERS of America, one of the Nation's largest and most formidable labor organizations.
UAW
From the Preamble to the UAW Constitution:
• The workers must be provided a meaningful voice in maintaining a safe and healthful workplace with decent working conditions, and must enjoy secured rights, together with a satisfactory standard of living and maximum job security.
• The workers must have a voice in their own destiny and the right to participate in making decisions that affect their own lives before such decisions are made.
• The UAW must play an active role at all levels of government to protect the lives and rights of its members and their families.
TAP TAP
• Union members must take seriously their responsibilities as citizens and work, through their union and individually, to realize the goals of participatory democracy and responsible and accountable government.

Formed in 1935 in Detroit, UAW made substantial gains in the labor movement with the sit down strike, famously at a Flint, Michigan GM plant. This cemented UAW's status as a major labor union and force to be reckoned with.

Panel from "Stick and stay, they're bound to pay"

By 1941, The UAW had unionized America's "Big Three" auto makers and later secured paid holidays, higher wages, pensions, and medical insurance for its members. UAW enjoyed years of growth and influence under president Walter Reuther, elected 1946.

There is no greater calling...
Than to serve your fellow man.

Reuther had a knack for stirring up animosity and opposition. He insisted that the industry open its books to demonstrate its alleged inability to meet wage demands.

C'mon!
lemme see!
No peeking!

Reuther believed that in order to be a successful bargaining agency, the UAW had to be able to uphold its side of the bargain. Wildcat strikes and disruptive behavior by union members had to be stopped by the union itself.

We must demonstrate that we are a disciplined, responsible organization; we not only have power, but we have power under control.

With Reuther at its head, the UAW expanded and fought alongside civil rights organizations to try and effect widesweeping social change.

The labor movement is about changing society.
What good is a dollar an hour more in wages if the neighborhood is burning down?

The UAW continued to enjoy a prosperous period through the 50s and 60s until Reuther's untimely death in 1970 in a plane crash.

In the early 1970s, changes in the global economy made it difficult for the UAW to unionize German and Japanese auto plants opening in the South. UAW membership began to decline.

As fuel prices rose, U.S. auto makers lost market share to foreign manufacturers selling fuel-efficient cars. Jobs were lost, and the UAW was forced to give up many of the benefits it had won for workers in the past.

No one is buying any cars!

I can't even afford the car I'm paid to build!

Much of the employment growth in the U.S. auto industry since 1980 was in non-union plants. By 2014, the UAW represented fewer than 400,000 workers.

Two-tier wages were first approved by the UAW in the late 1990s. In 2003 they entered the union's critical contracts with General Motors, Chrysler, and Ford.

In 2007, the second-tier wage program was expanded, intending to allow U.S. auto companies to hire new workers and become more competitive against Japanese and European transplants.

Following the 2007 Agreement, the base tier-two starting wage was lowered to about $15 per hour, lower than the average wage in non-union auto companies in the South. The unions were seen to provide a dubious advantage.

In the mid 1970s as membership declined, unions reached out to other industries in an attempt to diversify membership and boost their ranks. Strand was first organized at this time by District 65 and later UAW.

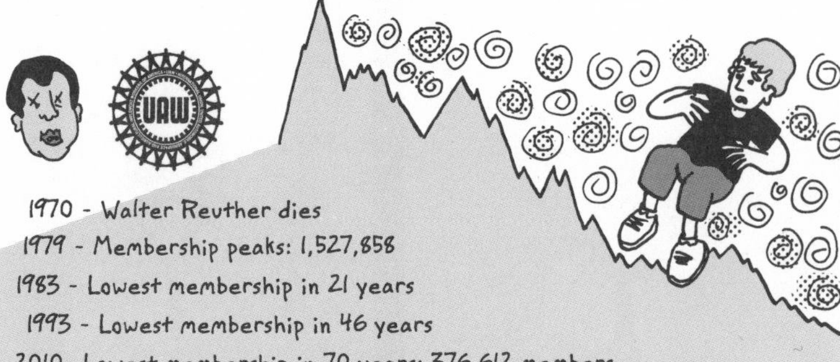

UAW
1970 - Walter Reuther dies
1979 - Membership peaks: 1,527,858
1983 - Lowest membership in 21 years
1993 - Lowest membership in 46 years
2010- Lowest membership in 70 years: 376,612 members.

The workers saw an opportunity to improve the store's working conditions, regulate management, and protect their earnings.

Not all employees at the time were interested. Some who worked more closely with Fred were decidedly pro-management, with open contempt for the workers. Others remained neutral.

As per the final agreement, the store would be able to designate a number of workers to be non-union managers, thus preserving the heirarchy.

While some of us have been employed at the Strand for decades, no current rank-and-file worker was hired prior to 1976—the year the store was first organized. Most workers at this time were fired or quit in the bitter aftermath of that first signing.

I worked there a month in the '90s in the warehouse upstairs, not on the floor.
Despite it being a union shop, I've worked in other non-union places with better working conditions.
The warehouse had bad ventilation, people got burned on the shrink wrap machine, and the pay wasn't even that great.
The shop steward worked up there with us, but was pretty lackadaisical. I felt I had to get out ASAP.
So I'm interested in hearing about others who stuck it out.

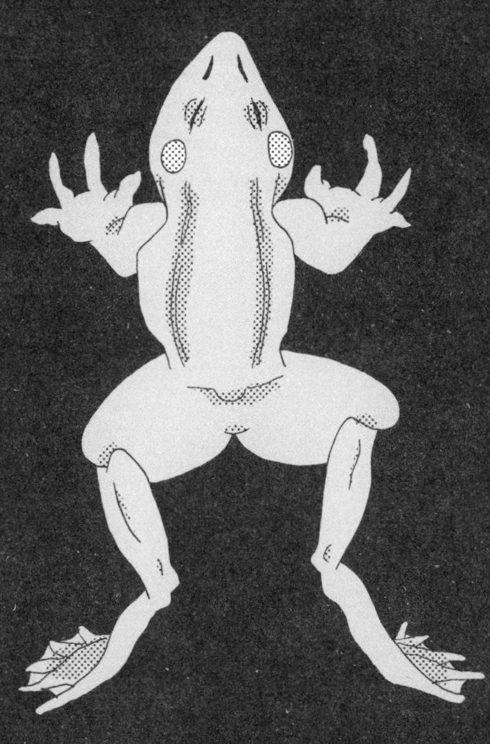

PART TWO

The whole store feels like an anachronism. More of a hobby than a profitable enterprise.

Any business that does its best to ditch older, experienced, high-salaried workers and replace them with young turnover types is sending up distress flares.

Both parties are acting in their own self-interest. I don't know how anyone can say that one party is more "right."

Every so often I read something that makes me realize how odd America looks from the UK. Here, the legal minimum leave is 28 days.

It's bullshit that workers are expected to cut back in "hard times" and take on the risk of running a business on behalf of the owners.

Workers demands are not always rational or viable. You know what they say about two tribes at war.

It's sort of the idea that the company keeps saying they are fucked and losing money, and that's why they need to stop paying us.

If it's really that bad, the management killed the store. They were at the helm of the ship that fucking crashed.

Maybe it's time for a new captain: worker control.

Somehow, the people in charge during what the company claims to be a downward spiral are left in place with no threat of cuts.

To leave them in charge would be irresponsible. The creation of a worker council would allow all workers of the store the ability to create their own task and labor.

Instantly, a more democratic workplace would be more efficient. With fewer manager salaries, it would save the company money.

New York City's Book Row: an area along fourth avenue between Astor Place and Broadway. Once home to as many as four dozen bookstores near the turn of the twentieth century.
4TH AVE

SALE

The patrons of book row valued books above all, and even moreso, a knowledge of books and the book market. A keen understanding of the trade set a seller apart.

Ah! Ze book iz rare but ze person who vill buy it iz rarer!

Indistinct among these bookshops was the Strand, opened in 1927 by Benjamin Bass with a 300 dollar loan and his own book collection as inventory.

I promise, I'll be able to pay you back... Some day.
This chap is straight baltic.

1929 saw the birth of his son, Fred, who began working the shop alongside his father at age 13, and eventually took over operations in 1956. Book row began to fade.

[It happened] because they didn't teach anybody anything.
They were strong, self-centered, competitive booksellers. They were protecting their knowledge, their turf.
Fred Bass

In the late 1950s, the store moved to its current location at 12 st. and Broadway. After decades of renting, Bass purchased the building for 8.2 million dollars.

Sale

You've come a long way, Bass!
I was gonna build a hotel on that spot!

OLD
RARE
NEW

BOOKS

With the initial proposal rejected, the company soon made clear its intention to continue negotiations upon their lawyer's return from vacation.

They voted it down ?! Idiots! BEEP
I gotta take this...
Hello? ... Nono, the Shiatsu. Right. And a ribeye.

The longer negotiations stall and matters go unsettled, the longer we workers go without definite benefits, while strife and tension pervade the workplace.

We've got a union, Buster!
UNION Buster
So do we.

In the meantime, the workers convene to discuss what we demand of management and possible actions we could take to ensure those demands are met.

I wannana... race truck!
(We often meet at bars)

Work slowdowns, sickouts, sit-ins, and work stoppages are all viable options with a contract in dispute (though it's in everyone's interest to avoid using them).

Next in line, please... or whatevs.

This is where the union–the members of the Union–depend most heavily on group actions and worker solidarity.

UAW tattoos
I think there's some room on my butt...

To affect change would require well-organized, mass participation despite a risk of repercussions from management or a possible objection or admonishment from our Union Local.

We are joined in our efforts by many supporters from outside the company.

Well-wishers, activists, political science majors from neighboring universities, and renegades from the nearby Occupy rallies are all eager to help our cause.

As we embrace their help, it becomes difficult to monitor or regulate actions taken by others in our name.

In March 2012, a group of outside supporters moving along Broadway surged into the store repeatedly shouting "Let Your Workers Unionize!"

The chant echoed briefly, turning heads in the immediate vicinity. The group was then forced to move on.

In April, a group of outside supporters disrupted a prominent book signing event, throwing a bundle of flyers into the crowd and denouncing them as

"Spectators!!"
Actually part of the event.

Many of us at Strand are rankled by these actions. Some of us defend it as part of a larger conversation of which we at Strand are only a small part.

Some of us advocate a more proactive stance in negotiations, a move away from the defensive in order to achieve our goals and accomplish real change.

Some have denounced the workers as spoiled or privileged, defending an ownership who is justifiably trying to cut costs in tough economic times.

I am not personally aligned with some of the means employed by our supporters in an effort to help, nor their "panty raid" mentality.

Their actions often target the wrong people, confuse those who we wish to inform, and potentially jeopardize the workers' livelihoods.

It wasn't him...
Same difference.

Ideally, our supporters would have all the facts, plan in cooperation with all involved, and proceed with a careful, calculated, democratically approved course of action in our collective favor.

But this could result in gridlock and inaction, or put us at a tactical disadvantage. Not even this comic is in keeping with those ideals.

The union is nebulous, with wide diversity in feelings and opinions. Should those not in keeping with the majority be ignored or disregarded?

Or should each member be given the freedom to impact their situation by any method they choose, in what they perceive to be their own best interest?

And should this freedom extend to those outside our union? It's easy to antagonize, defame, or humiliate the company under the pretense of "The Greater Good"...

...When you feel safe in knowing that someone else will carry the consequences.

But there is heartening evidence that a small group of workers united, acting in their own self interest can incite change. NYC, 1991:

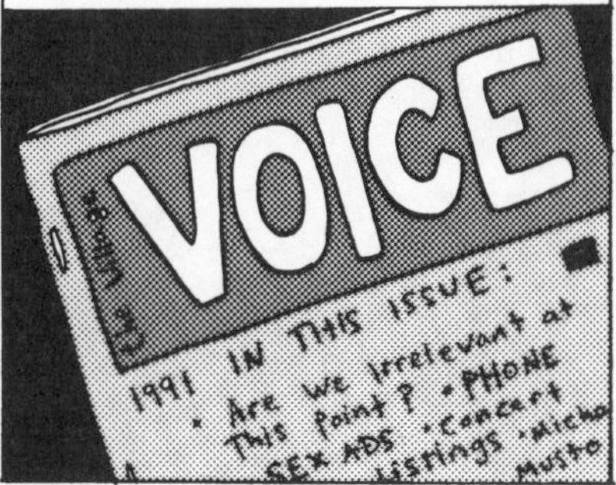

The *Village Voice* reports a conflict at the Strand in which sixteen workers were suspended after a tussle in the building's lobby with owner Fred Bass.

I think I'm about to do something crazy.

Workers at the time were affiliated with District 65, which was running a deficit in its medical insurance program. Workers had lost their pharmaceutical coverage.

Couldn't afford anti-biotics
Couldn't afford birth control
Couldn't afford Prozac

The Local requested Bass pay $51,000 to augment his contribution to the program, thus restoring coverage to his workers. Bass resisted.

"I'm getting ripped off!
I'm paying all this money, and it's no good to you."
Fred Bass circa 1990

Some felt Bass was manipulating the situation to try and discredit or eliminate the union entirely. On March 21, 1991, 18-20 workers confronted Bass and accused him of stalling negotiations.

Nancy Bass, his daughter, then an employee at the store, was allegedly shoved amidst the tumult, while some accounts have her punching an employee while opening a door.

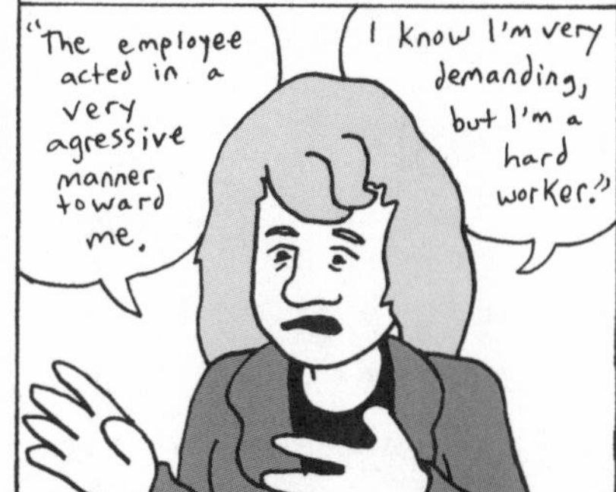

"The employee acted in a very agressive manner toward me.
I know I'm very demanding, but I'm a hard worker."

After the incident, Fred agreed to pay the $51,000.

Worker Power!
Don't leave me hangin' bro!
A "pound"

Today, Fred Bass is in his mid-eighties and Nancy is part owner of the store. Storewide, major changes are underway.

We've monetized every inch of this place...
Charge the mice rent!

Some predict a corporate sell out of the brand for continued operation, in which case a unionized work force could diminish its value to a buyer.

We're prepared to offer you...
They never broke the union...
Five million dollars!
10 Million $

Others envision a Strand closure, and conversion of the space (Owned by Bass as Bass Realty LLC.) to be rented out to a separate retail entity.

Flip ya for it.

As the Bass family owns both the Strand and the building at 12 St. and Broadway in which it operates, their livelihood is not subject to the whims of dollar sign-eyed NYC landlords and cartoonishly outsized rent-hikes.

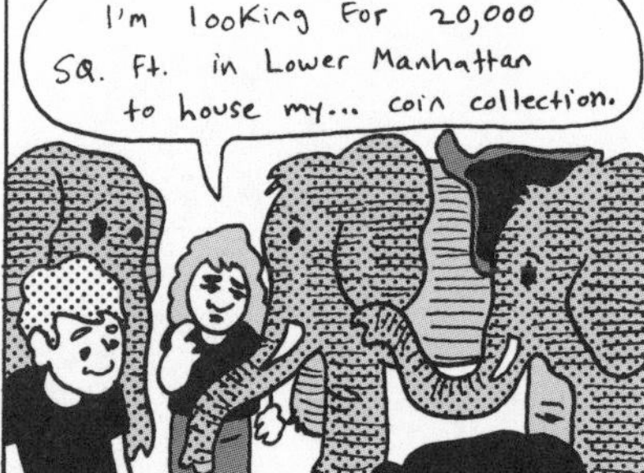

I'm looking for 20,000 Sq. Ft. in Lower Manhattan to house my... coin collection.

It's possible the proposed givebacks are the early phase of a long term strategy to weaken and nullify the union, as opposed to a means to compensate for their loss of revenue in a harsh business climate.

"In Store (Sales) are up eight* percent!"
* November 2011 Interview Also Panel 4:6

THE STRAND BOOK TOTE

Introduced in 1970, the Strand Book Tote is an internationally recognized NYC icon. To date there have been countless designs and variations of the bag, including an "artists" series designed by cartoonists Dan Clowes, Art Spiegelman, David Hockney, and others.

The bag's simple design and NY literary cache have made it popular among NYers, some carrying their bag well beyond the limits of its durability.

STRAND
TACO KIT

The Book tote is the forerunner of the Strand logo cottage industry, which today features an array of branded products, from coffee mugs to dog onesies and "everything in between."

BZZ BZZ

STRAND
MADE IN CHINA

Dude, think your phone's ringing.

BZZ BZZ

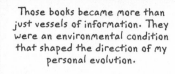

For better or worse, my father's library had a very profound impact on who I am.

Those books became more than just vessels of information. They were an environmental condition that shaped the direction of my personal evolution.

Aside from the books on their shelves, were those handfuls of books scattered about the house. A copy of *Ulysses* in the living room...

...or a Feynman book at the dinner table. New worlds of knowledge and information became unintimidating and an everyday part of my life.

I love being a bookseller. I am proud to be a bookseller. I've wondered if I can afford to remain in this profession, though.

The greatest minds of our future generations will be shaped by their environment, and I want to make sure books remain a part of that environment.

I have been with the store for four and a half years. I voted to accept the previous contract.
I worked at the Annex until it closed in 2008. Then I was transferred to the basement of the main store.
Not knowing the challenge it would bring, I chose to be a union steward.
I could help by being an informed witness.
The Rare Book Room was an opportunity to advance. I learned how little opportunity for advancement there is.
I majored in journalism at a small liberal arts college in Missouri, and I am writing several fiction stories and a novel.
I was honored to be placed on the negotiating committee but it left me tired and stressed, like I am playing a game with no set rules...

I am the son of a small business owner!
Since 1978, my father has made a reliable living selling pop-culture memorabilia such as movie posters, baseball cards, books, 45s, LPs, 8x10s, pez, porn, comics, toys, ephemera, and myriad other curious artifacts from his store in Huntington, Long Island.

Growing up, the store was home. I would spend time there after school and on weekends.

My first job was for my Dad, organizing LIFE magazines by cover date. As compensation, I was given a few dollars, lunch, and some Archie comic books.

I wonder if these skills will be handy in my future...

Over the course of 30 years, rising rents and a changing business landscape have forced the business to relocate a number of times, edging ever toward the fringes...

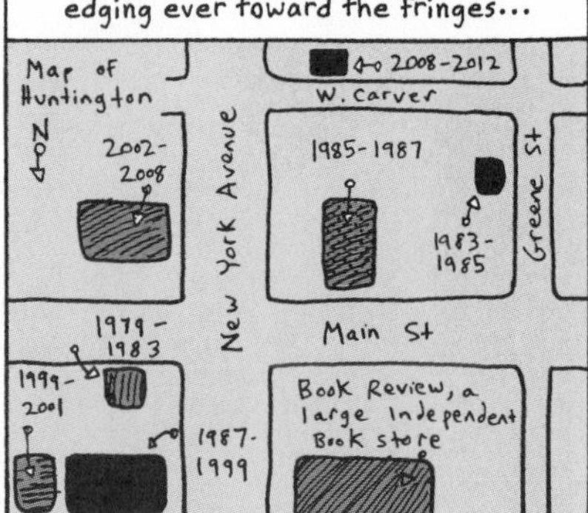

...as the town of Huntington became a hotspot of high-end nail salons and restaurants. My family's store soon disappeared from the map entirely.

Looks great! – But how do I wipe my butt?

eBay and internet commerce were first seen as a boon to both the dealer and collector.

Any item, anywhere, at a market dictated price. Soon, eBay was the go-to place for anything from priceless collectibles to garage sale leftovers.

Trade show, catalog, and walk-in sales dwindled with the rise of digital retail, and as a result of store closings, towns and cities became "Disneyfied" and homogenized.

Old establishments still using the old model were caught off-guard as they began losing customers to cheaper, more convenient retail outlets.

In New York City, unique, community businesses (including countless Lower East Side record shops) saw their days numbered...

...leaving once culturally rich areas, like St. Marks Place between Second and Third Avenues, as little more than an outdoor mall and food court.

Businesses were forced to branch out, assimilate, water down their brand, or close.

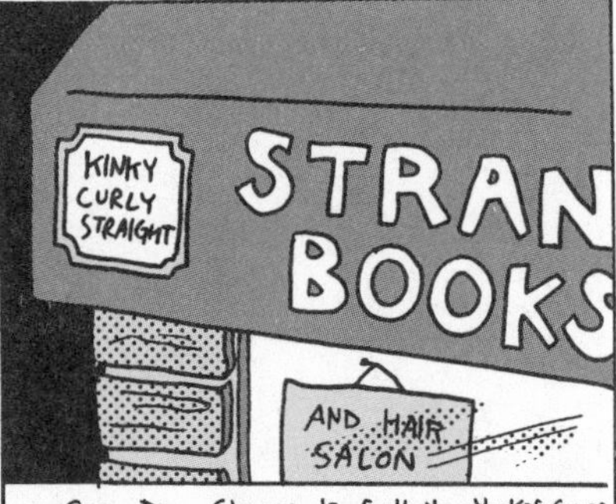

Another obstacle faced by those dealing used, rare, or fetishized collectables is the aging out of the collector.

For some, the impetus to collect is rooted in nostalgia. What will people be nostalgic for in another 50 years?

When a thing is digitized, the concepts of scarcity, condition, propriety, vintage, and intrinsic monetary value no longer apply.

Some may argue in favor of a move away from material abundance and those looking to capitalize on our nostalgia, but this is not the same as us overcoming the human desire to HAVE THINGS.

In some instances, It becomes not a matter of a means through which to fulfill demand, but rather that the demand may soon not exist.

A Lone Ranger collectible, for instance, nostalgically resonant to someone in their sixties, will likely be worthless outside a historical context in a generation or two.

To a post-digital generation, these physical relics are obsolete; A burden, along with the businesses that traffic them. These businesses are fighting for their lives.

Many "brick and mortar" booksellers, such as Strand, partner themselves with online competitors like Amazon to boost their online book sales. But they are at the mercy of Amazon's rules and prices.

Retail outlets become "Amazon Showrooms." The public demands of low price and immediacy make it difficult for a smaller business with fewer employees to compete.

A once reasonable two-week shipping timeframe becomes interminable. A half-price, used paperback is suddenly deemed unaffordable.

Amazon made its reputation selling books at minimal cost, then branched out, selling everything under the sun to better cater to the needs of its growing customer base.

As Amazon extends its reach into areas such as book publishing, it could effectively limit the exchange of information on a worldwide scale,

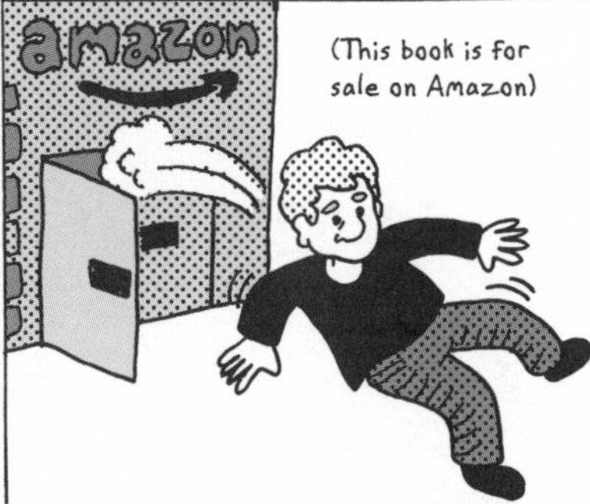

Amazon's strict standards and seller policies inhibit commerce, making it difficult or impossible for small, independent businesses to survive.

One area in which traditional retail establishments can compete with massive online conglomerates is, of course, customer service...

...by having a knowledgable, enthusiastic workforce on hand to engage customers and promote sales.

The workers of the Strand are what connect it to the community, a connection It needs in order to ensure its continued relevance and competitive edge.

We, the workers, provide a social interface in a commodified form, which is our labor; the commodity necessary for all others to subsist.

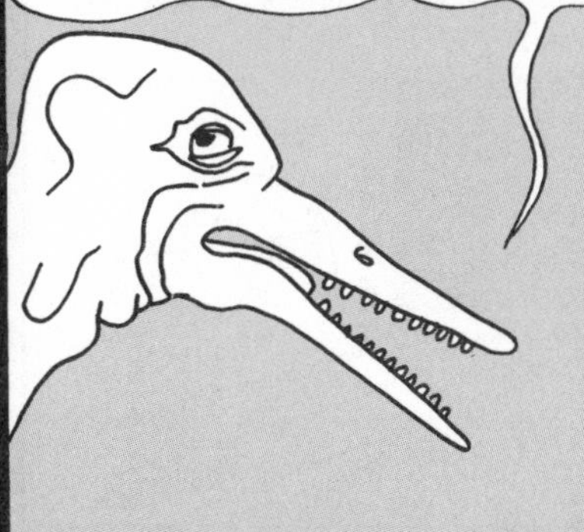
When I started at the Strand, I had no idea what kind of shit I was getting myself into.

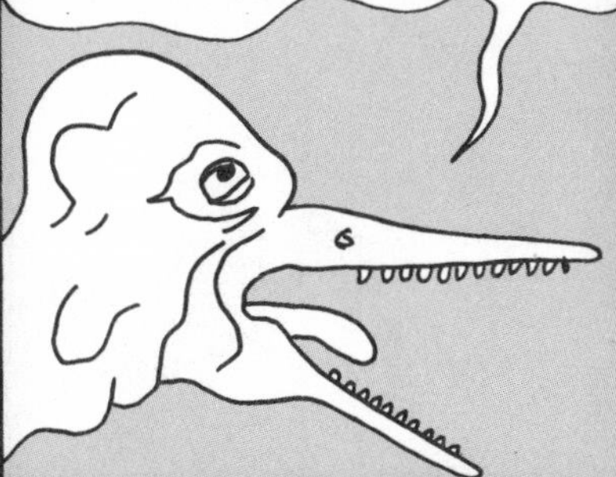
I learned about the union struggle and felt inclined to stand in solidarity with my coworkers, even though I was not yet protected by the union.

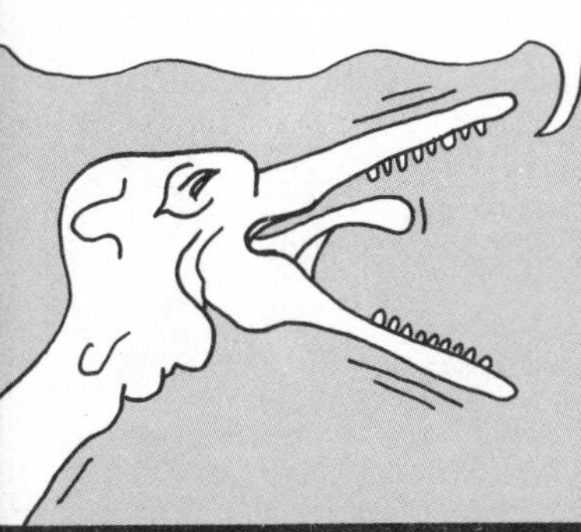
Right is right and wrong is wrong, and if you don't stand against what's wrong, you're just part of the force that allows the wrong to continue.

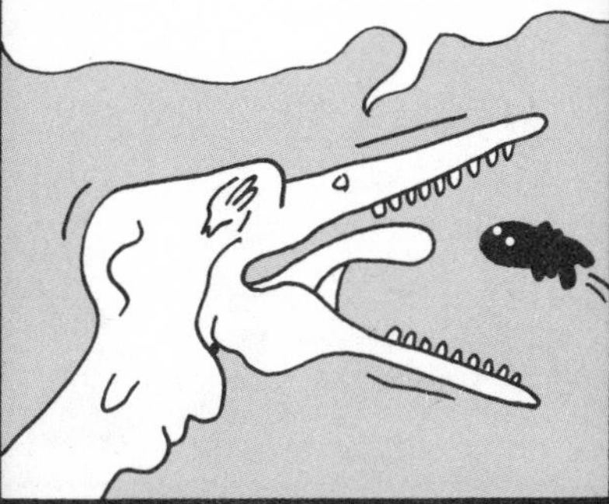
As a new worker, I felt like a pawn in a game in which management was trying to intimidate the unionized workers. It was uncomfortable.

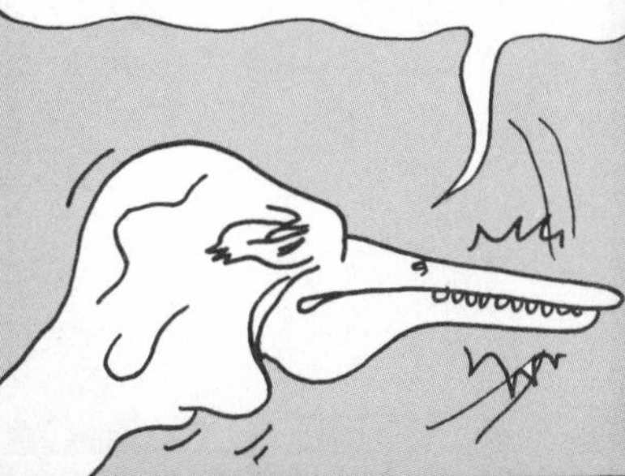
I was fired after three weeks, but not before attending worker meetings and giving an anonymous interview to the press, in which I expressed support for my unionized coworkers.

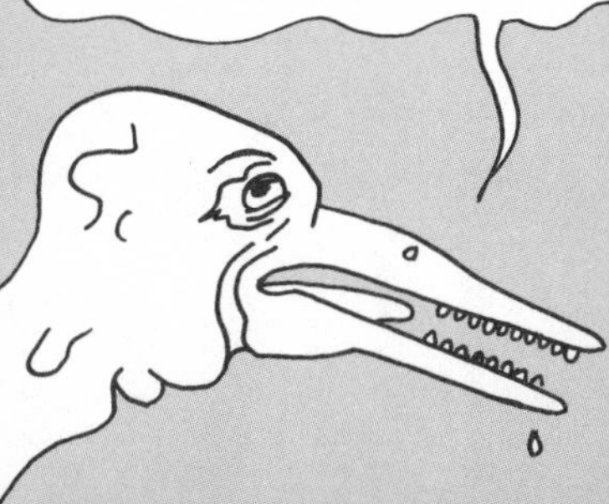
It sucks not getting a regular paycheck, but I don't appreciate feeling as though I am being used as a tactic to scare other workers.

STRAND
STRAND
STRAND BOOKSTORE
OLD RARE NEW
STRAND BOOKSTORE

PART THREE

Ahhh...

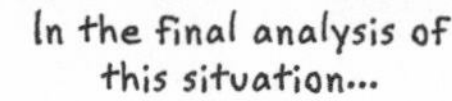
In the final analysis of
this situation...

It shall take organization
and mobilization
as a solution!

Nihil tenendum est*!

*fear
nothing

May 1, a workers' holiday, otherwise known as May Day, or International Workers' Day.

Worldwide, people demonstrate their dissatisfaction with a system in which the rights of banks and businesses come before their own.

No work, no school, no shopping, no banking. A one day general strike of the world's workers...

...a concerted effort to show these institutions how much they rely on us to cooperate, and what would happen should we refuse to comply.

Throughout New York city, a full schedule of pickets, protest, and marches was planned, culminating in a parade down Broadway to a mass rally in Union Square.

The Strand is ideally situated mere blocks from the action, a prime spot where we could appeal to the crowdsurge and raise awareness.

Word of a sick-out spread among the unionized staff. Enthusiasm was high. Participation in the general strike was encouraged.

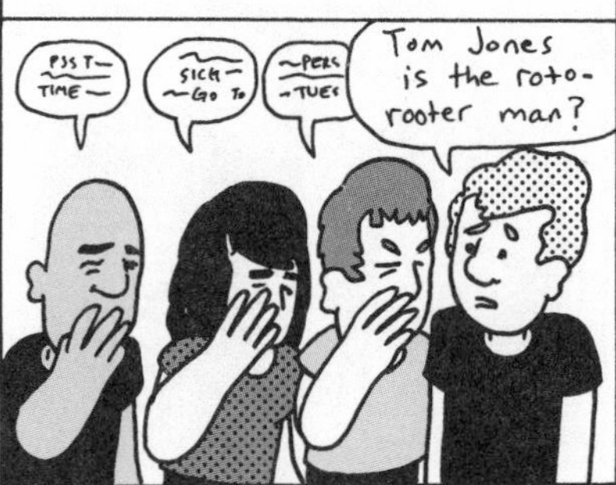

We would send management the message that we were united, that we disapproved of their treatment of us, and that we had the power to impede the day-to-day function of the store at our will.

Our Local could not openly condone a sick-out action. Instead, they organized a rally to take place outside the store to coincide with the march down Broadway.

Those who opted to work that day could join the line on their lunchbreak or flaunt their solidarity while on the sales floor.

Many had been planning for months to participate in the general strike actions, both Strand-specific and city-wide.

I was initially on the fence about the whole thing, and remained undecided until just days before.

Managerial decisions made in the days leading up to May Day would indicate that they had been preparing for a possible sick-out or strike.

With convenient timing, workers involved in union activity were promoted to manager, thus neutralizing their role in the union and securing one more body on the sales floor.

Likewise, an inordinate number of new workers were hired and trained across all departments.

These workers were not protected by our union contract. There is a three-month probationary period for all new-hires during which time they are susceptible to termination.

They could be fired at anytime, no cause need be supplied.

If I were I to join the sick-out, wouldn't I be leaving our new comrades in the lurch to shoulder an overwhelming workload?

Would I be singled out by management as one of a few rabble-rousers and subjected to petty, indirect retribution?

As May Day approached, my concerns proved misguided. Several of the new hires were aware of the situation at the store...

...sympathetic to the nature of the day, and wise to their precarious role in the conflict.

Moreover, it was a slow, tuesday afternoon.

May 1: No one could know what to expect. The city was tense, as were we at the Strand.

We gathered that afternoon with representatives from our union local to distribute placards and bolster our resolve.

Then, at 3 PM, dozens of workers and our supporters swarmed the corner of 12th and Broadway, surrounding the store and blocking its entrances.

Chants of "Union Busting—it's disgusting" and

NANCY BASS, YOU'RE RICH AND RUDE! WE DON'T LIKE YOUR ATTITUDE!

were accompanied by a full marching band and the cacophony of nearby protests and rallies.

Curious onlookers offered their support. Others were recruited from the crowds amassing at Union Square.

Friends, former employees, and even customers jumped in line, swelling our ranks. A number of reporters and photographers were on hand documenting it all.

Customers trying to sell back their books were chased off, and loading docks blocked, effectively shutting down the store's operation—

Managers were seen grousing in high up windows like cartoon villains while their customers were prevented from shopping.

At 4 PM the crowd dispersed, with management left to survey the aftermath, glaring disapprovingly at any straggling employees.

The day's action was successful. We showed the owners the extent of our powers united as a workforce and our essential function in the running of the store.

Their response:

Yesterday was a demonstration. People exercised their first amendment rights and the Strand supports independent spirits.

The management at Strand treat us like children.
I don't know how everyone else reacts, but I find myself feeling like a kid.
Nervous. Hoping for approval. Hoping I won't be punished.
The picketing on May Day made me feel like I was making them nervous for a change.
Made me feel like I didn't have anything to be afraid of.
It was fun, exciting, and a long time coming.

Starting sometime this week, the art department managers will begin to schedule lunches.

No longer will you be allowed to eat when you are hungry or need a break...

...because someone else will make that decision for you.

No longer will there exist a conversation or a discussion between two people to reach a mutually agreeable solution.

The second party has been removed from the conversation altogether.

This is what is happening. We are being removed from the conversation.

Managers may have a perfectly reasonable sounding rationale for scheduling lunch breaks. And it might seem like ultimately not a big deal.

But we're adults. Shouldn't we decide for ourselves when we have lunch, or even if we have lunch at all?

Whatever management's rationale may be, our dignity is a strong, compelling counter argument.

What if we were arguing over a more obviously "hands-off" area, like our sex lives—If management, for instance, insisted we only date non-employees.

The obnoxiousness of the demand would seem intolerable and there probably wouldn't really even be an argument.

But in either case, it's not arguments that decide the matter. It's how much we, the workers, value our dignity and what we are willing to do to preserve it.

It's a tough decision to publish these comics.
Thankfully, each installment has been met with general enthusiasm, and I consider them artistically successful in their own right.
Ben
Andrea
Gary
Estelle
Jimmy
Rico

I am new to Comics Journalism; unfamiliar with the intricacies of labor politics and contract negotiation.

I am learning at both, helped along by generous friends, regardless of their own opinions on the matter at hand.

These comics have opened a dialogue from which those involved or interested can deepen their understanding of these matters.

Among those who participate in the dialogue is the company itself.

While I aim to be prudent in presenting these ideas, and I can likely not be directly fired on the sole grounds of having published these comics,

I could still be looked upon unfavorably by management or my coworkers, thus compromising a pleasant work environment.

These comics draw attention to me where I was once largely anonymous, potentially subjecting my workplace actions to harsher scrutiny.

It is not beyond the legal means of the company to have me squeezed out, or to make the day-to-day job so unbearable that I quit.

So, am I willing to jeopardize workplace harmony to gamble on minor public notoriety and a few decent, if helpful comics?

And if not, am I on some level committing to work at the Strand indefinitely?

Is it even possible to support oneself solely on a career in comics?

Comics are not immune to the same economic forces that negatively impact the Strand as a bookseller, and other small businesses in general.

Cash-strapped publishers are wary to chance breaking new artists. We are expected to work for free, with promise of "Exposure" as compensation. Creators are devalued along with what they create.

Published authors receive low rates with no benefits or guarantees. Essentially their own chronic interns, artists are caught in a cycle of low-pay work, with small hope of a steady job prospect in their field.

Of course, the issue at Strand goes beyond what I want for me and my comics. We are each concerned for our own livelihoods, and while the comics may be a means to an end, they are hardly an end in themselves.

At best, these comics can raise awareness, and illuminate our struggle...

...and in the future provide an indelible record of events from which to learn and improve one's own situation.

I'll admit, I am sometimes conflicted in my desires. A beneficial resolution to the conflict may not yield the most dramatic climax to my comic tale.

A strike would make for potent drama but be terrible for the workers. In the end, our victory over management will be a triumph of the underdog—a boon to the livelihoods of the workers and a satisfying conclusion for the reader...

Or as the case may be, the anti-climax of our quiet defeat will leave many of us disenchanted and confused.

Previous installments of this comic have sparked minor controversy among workers, winning support from some for what others consider inappropriate, or a strategic misstep.

This only goes to underscore the diversity of opinion among even a small, like-minded sampling of Strand staff.

It's a diversity we should be especially mindful of with negotiations afoot, and an imminent staff-wide vote on the horizon determining our fate.

Some members of the group take for granted that the other 100 or more Strand constituents not typically present at meetings agree with them on the issues at hand.

But the votes do not reflect this. While it is true that the initial contract proposal was voted down in April 2012 by an "overwhelming majority"...

There were still, unbelievably, a number of people who voted in its favor!

Why were some compelled to approve a contract under the terms of which we were sure to lose,

when a vote against it posed no risk whatsoever and could, with time and persistence, reap great rewards? How can we prevent a future upset of this nature?

Our ages range decades, our origins span continents, and our interests are as varied as the books we sell.

What's good for Ben may not be good for Andrea.

They have wildly different concerns and perspectives.

Some of us depend on our benefits to get by. Some see this job as a stopgap until that real opportunity comes, hoping that when it does it can support us...

and still others may just not care. All have equal votes. It is important that the active members of the union keep in mind this diversity

and extend our "inreach" as far as possible, to preserve the long term interests of the union at large.

I've worked in three clothing stores. Selling clothes and books are wildly different but the common thing that I've experienced is meeting great people who often turn into great friends.

While the circumstance of our prolonged contract negotiations is less than ideal, the experience has made me not just thankful to know them but very proud to be working with them.

Whether it be organizing, articles, picketing, posters, zines, or comics, the staff demonstrates itself to be an awesome crew of characters, and an inspiring, empowered set of motherfuckers.

The willingness to fight back in these ways is something I have not had the opportunity to experience at other retail workplaces.

We worked under no contracts and management was always quick to remind us of how easily and quickly we could be replaced. We always felt powerless and resentful.

Being at the Strand has not only shown me the value of union membership, but how crucial it is to fight with my coworkers for the treatment, respect, and contract we deserve.

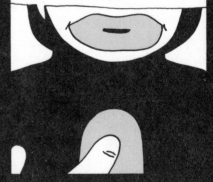

It seems like a lot of what the managers do at Strand is check up on us, and try their hardest to appease upper management.

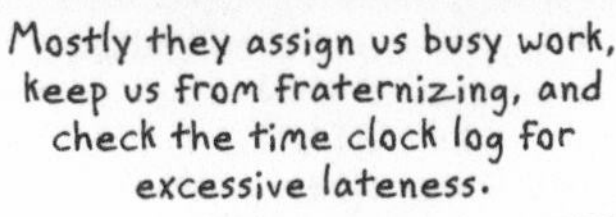

Mostly they assign us busy work, keep us from fraternizing, and check the time clock log for excessive lateness.

More or less, they babysit.
They treat us like we're children, projecting on to us their own need to be babysat all the way up the line.

If a manager at any level is petty or behaves towards me like I'm a child, that's fine.

But that's childish behavior on their part. I refuse to participate.

I'm an adult and I behave as such, in and out of the store.
So, someone else's hang-ups?
It doesn't really bother me.
I can sleep.

You can't afford it.
$

PART FOUR

I worked at Strand from 2004-2009. I served as a shop steward and participated in the 2007 negotiations.

My new job is good but there's no union. I haven't had a raise in a year and a half, though my rent has been raised twice in that time.

I couldn't afford insurance for years. I've only just started treating back problems I've had for over a year.

The toe I broke two years ago went completely untreated. Still, I need this job and the fact that I could be fired for no reason whatsoever keeps me up at night.

Every time a union is crushed by misguided management, it gets harder for the rest of us to keep our heads above water.

The struggle at Strand belongs to all of us. Solidarity, motherfuckers!

As a contrarian intellectual arriving in The City during recession, I was lucky to land a job 10 years ago at the Strand.

Burdened with student debt & lacking any means, I was thankful for the pitiful $7.50/hr. which could not even pay my bills.

Being a penniless communist homosexual atheist made me persona non grata to much of American society.

Thankfully the Strand was a space willing to use my talents regardless of these exigencies.
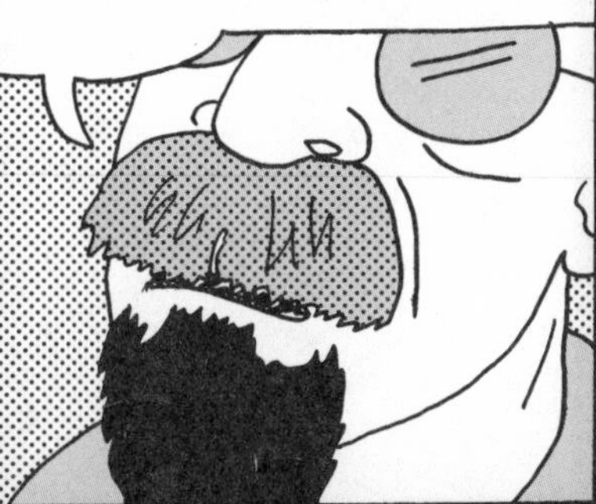
Because I have found labor I love, it is now my perpetual duty to defend those I love— my coworkers.

As soon as I could, I became a shop steward and threw myself fully into the struggle for justice vis-a-vis what were now my people.

The terms and conditions of our employment by the Strand are determined by a collective bargaining agreement between UAW Local 2179 and the Strand.

This agreement defines wages, raises, health insurance and our weekly contribution to it, personal days, vacation time, and holiday pay among other things. It is commonly referred to as "the contract."

The specifics of the contract are determined in collective bargaining (or negotiations) between the union and the store.

During negotiations, the company is represented by management and lawyers. Although Fred Bass used to negotiate for himself, the role of management has been assumed by Eddie Sutton, and Fred's lawyer, Harry Burstein.

The union is represented by a committee of Strand workers referred to as the negotiating committee or bargaining committee...

...as well as officers of Local 2179, Usually Vice-President Vilma Torres-Mulholland and President Pablo Valcarcel.

The committee is usually four to six workers, often, but not exclusively, shop stewards.

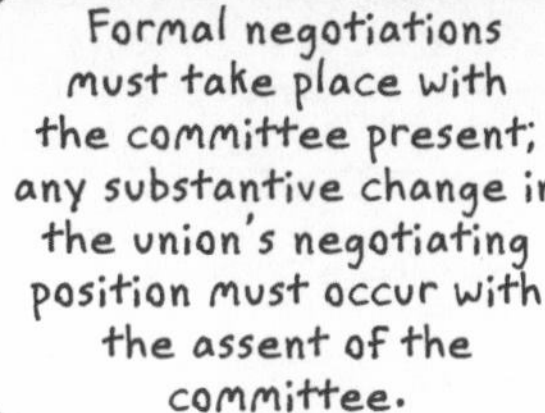

Formal negotiations must take place with the committee present; any substantive change in the union's negotiating position must occur with the assent of the committee.

As the only workers witness to the proceedings, the committee will be the workers' main source of information during negotiations.

When a deal is presented to the membership for ratification, the committee may or may not endorse the agreement.

Given the number of individuals participating in negotiations, meetings can be difficult to schedule. It is common for negotiating sessions to be separated by weeks at a time.

When the two sides meet, each presents its proposal for changes to the contract.

The law requires that both sides "bargain in good faith." Neither party can make impossible or absurd demands.

Neither party can refuse to negotiate altogether. Neither can dig in its heels and refuse to make any concessions at all. If either side drops or changes an item, that side cannot reverse course in the future.

For example, if the union asked for twelve personal days initially and then changed our proposal to ten, we could not go back up to eleven or twelve.

Anything said at the negotiating table can be binding. This forbids speculative offers. In other words, neither side could say "If we were to give up X, would you give up Y?"

Because of this stricture, it is permissible for Pablo and Eddie to step out of the room and conduct "closed door" sessions.

Although the content of such sessions is unknown, any subsequent action at the table requires the assent of the negotiating committee.

Negotiating sessions involve some amount of confidentiality, for both legal and tactical reasons.

The committee, being the only Strand workers at the table, will function as the eyes, ears, and voice of all the workers.

It is thus imperative that the committee be aware of and responsive to the concerns of the workers as a whole.

The hardest and most important job of the committee is to listen to and educate all of the workers. This requires distribution of information by any means possible. Flyers, newsletters, meetings, emails, etc.

But, literature unread and meetings unattended are worthless. We must all be engaged, attentive, and critical.

The committee can be more effective if it understands and speaks for the workers united. We must all read and listen and then speak our minds, for the ignorance or silence of the people destroys democracy.

This strip was distributed among the workers of the Strand in the weeks leading up to a strike authorization vote.
It's not a strike!
BOOKS NOT CROOKS!
UAW
USED RARE NUDE
STRAN
BOOKS

What complicates the process of disseminating information among the constituents is that, simply, we do not know who they all are.

Lolly?
It's okay. I'm your co-worker.

A fervent outside supporter of our efforts at Strand has continually urged:

Get the email, phone number, and schedule of every worker.
You need to have this info if you ever hope to be organized.

Her advice on how best to accomplish this:

Just go to the bar! Have drinks with everybody!

The Strand employs approximately 150 unionized workers at four locations in two boroughs, with little interaction between them.

Hey, I need a book transfer.
You got the ISBN?

How can we get personal information of someone whose name we don't know, who we have never met, and who we have no way of accounting for?
Confuscious say: You can't prove a negative.
Extra fortu
Double lucky

Our bylaws state that the Local must provide this information to the stewards. However, despite our repeated requests and some recent showing of support on their part, they have yet to do so.
Okay, so now the next step is...
Remember when we helped with the picket?

The workers took it upon themselves to try and compile this list. It remains woefully incomplete.
This guy didn't specify his email server.
Just put GMail.
He's 43
Hot mail

Surely, it should be easy enough for our UAW local, part of a large international organization, to print a list of names of those who pay them 3% of their wages as dues.
Did you get us that list?
That information is confidential, but good luck!

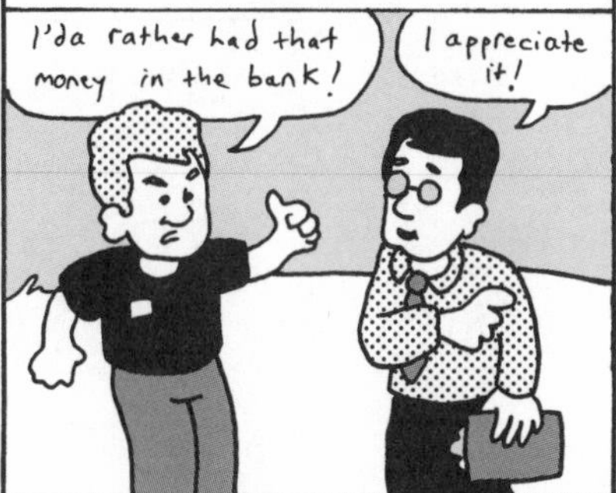
This is one of many ways that some workers feel that the local fails to deserve those dues, which, for many of us, total thousands of dollars and counting.
I'da rather had that money in the bank!
I appreciate it!

In January 2012, the local agreed to a reduced healthcare package which would save money for the company by increasing our pharmaceutical co-pays and limiting coverage.
My birth control costs $90 now! I can't afford it any more!

A clause in our standing contract stipulates that the company must continue to provide the same or a "comparable" health plan, allowing them to switch providers at any time.

Still, the local did little to prevent the switch to what was clearly an inferior plan...

...and failed to notify the workers or stewards until after the change had already been put into effect.

More recently, the local botched the negotiations that resulted in the store's inadequate final offering.

Negotiations which, shockingly, were conducted without counsel on our behalf.

A meeting at the union office was held just prior to our vote on that contract, at which constituents were granted an audience with UAW President Pablo Valcarcel.

Pablo was confrontational, condescending, and seemingly misunderstanding of the terms of the contract or trying to confuse the workers with doublespeak.

Having never seen their financial records, he urged us to bend over and accept what was offered...

...siding with management on their claims that Amazon and E-books are hurting their once thriving business.

He warned against a strike, suggested the situation was beyond our control, and demonstrated what some felt was a lack of either leadership skills, interest in us as a group, or the magnitude of his position.

The terms of the contract pressed upon us at that time would effectively dissolve the strength of this constituency, the local's largest, in just a few short years.

Isn't it in their best interest as well as ours to preserve and encourage the enduring power of our union?

It's not a strike!

This is all messed up. If everyone only looks out for themselves, everyone will lose.

Obviously I'm opposed to it, but I can't fault management or ownership for what they are trying to do.

They're just doing their job. It's not surprising that they want to get as much money for themselves as they can.

The workers are scared. Look what we're up against. I'm disappointed in them sometimes, but I can't be mad at them.

Besides, we're fighting this on our own time. Our job is to sell books. Thats what we get paid for and we show up every day and we do it.

Who I'm really mad at is the Local. Their job is to support the workers. I don't feel like they're doing their job properly.

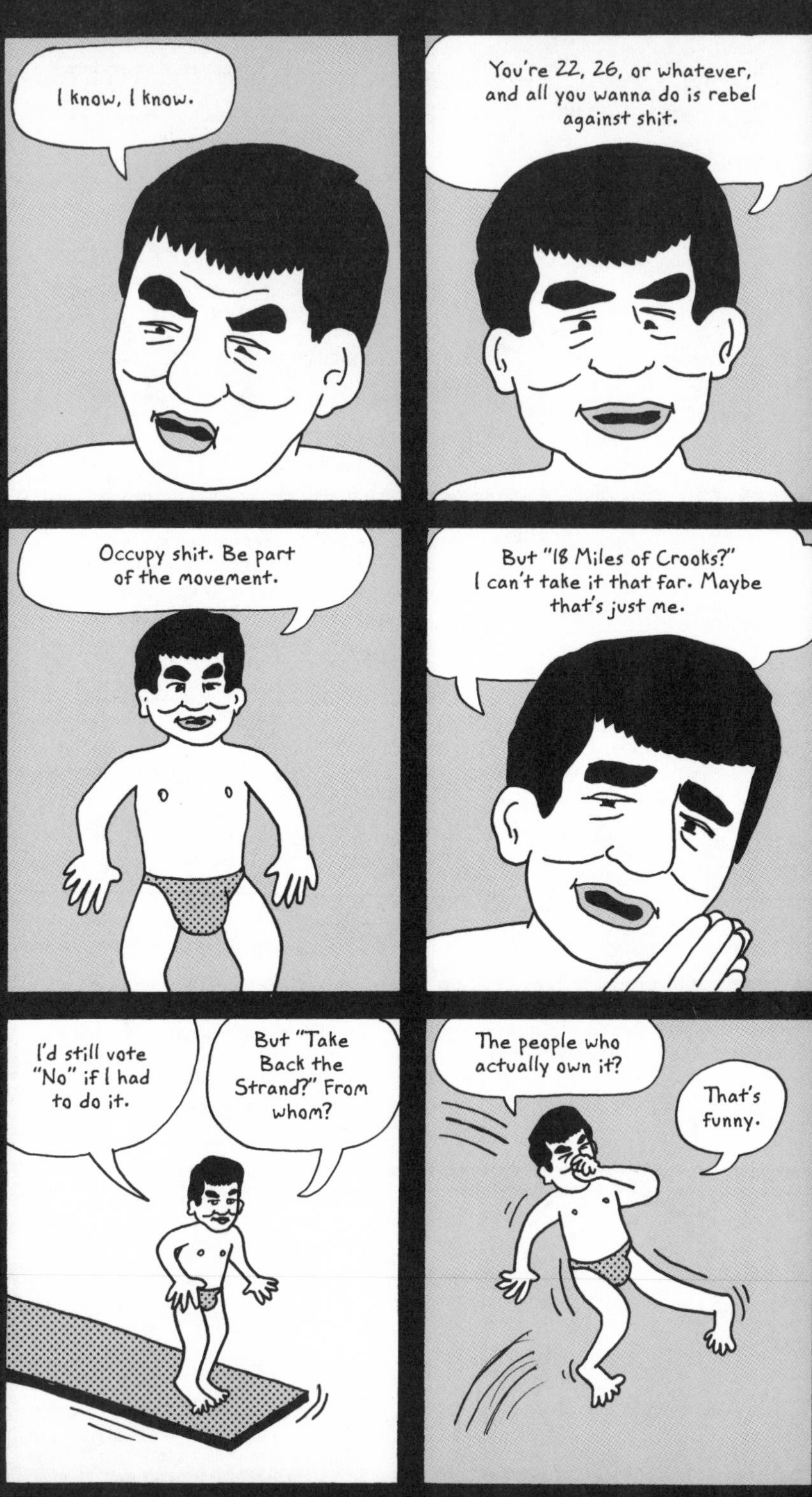
I know, I know.
You're 22, 26, or whatever, and all you wanna do is rebel against shit.
Occupy shit. Be part of the movement.
But "18 Miles of Crooks?" I can't take it that far. Maybe that's just me.
I'd still vote "No" if I had to do it.
But "Take Back the Strand?" From whom?
The people who actually own it?
That's funny.

Among the workers there is a small, open group who meet regularly to share information and discuss further actions in our continuing struggle.

The group is not officially appointed, nor is it represented or bound by the union local in any capacity.

I'm not in any way qualified to help. In fact, my participation may be a detriment to the proceedings.

Welcome aboard!

We meet and act in our own interest, in the way we best see fit to ensure a beneficial resolution to our workplace conflict.

There are a core few at the heart of the group, though all workers are encouraged to join and contribute. Attendance has been dwindling as the conflict drags on.

Dissatisfied with recent efforts, some have denounced the group as "theater" and openly question our purpose.

The group is mainly important at this stage because it keeps us united and reenforces our solidarity.

Earlier in this book, I expressed my disapproval of actions taken by outside supporters in our interest.

I was outraged, as were others, that we were not consulted, nor was our approval sought during the planning stages, even though we would likely bear the brunt of any repercussions.

Our reaction was seen as divisive within our group and made many of the outside supporters hesitant or unwilling to further assist us.

Those actions were determined and approved by the same group of workers, mentioned above, with which I was not yet involved. I started attending meetings and becoming active some time later.

I now find myself eagerly planning similar actions, confident in their righteousness and necessitude...

...all while wondering how people not present at the planning meeting and unaware of the process will react to the decisions made.

While the group can be slow to move, ineffective, and sometimes irrelevant, as is the case with most democracies/bureaucracies...

...it is hard to deny the effectiveness of certain actions planned specifically and exclusively at these meetings. They are not held in vain:

Few actions work against our goal and we should encourage and embrace the efforts of anyone according to their abilities.

Often when brought to the group, even a minor idea is dissected and analyzed so thoroughly that all parties lose interest or are turned off by the end.

In the event a lone employee acts with swift personal decisiveness, these actions can come under scrutiny after the fact, discouraging such behavior in the future.

Worse, when an idea is proposed, agreed upon, and a person or persons appointed to carry it out, it sometimes goes undone, and is subsequently swept under the rug, never to be discussed again.

The union local is discouraging of our efforts. They take a hard line against any actions except what has been approved and organized by their office.

Often, these actions are benign and more symbolic than truly effective, leaving us to impotently await the company's next move.

As always, the spread of information among the workers and to the public is a valuable tool relative to its risk and cost.

At one point, I took it upon myself to design and have printed a cache of flyers to be distributed to the public.

Upon seeing the flyers, the local expressed their disapproval and supplied a list of changes and demands.

One of which was the inclusion of two separate union logos in the design as well as several other nit-picky "suggestions."

I wondered why the local had any jurisdiction over what we spent our personal time and money producing. Meanwhile the group seemed to be dissuaded from using the flyers.

Although of minor significance, the situation made me withdraw and re-allocate my energies, a reaction likely shared by those who offered their help to us in the past, only to be scorned.

In order to affect real, or any change, it seems actions must be taken individually in conjunction with group efforts.

The group must follow through and streamline its focus, consulting the local only when necessary, relegating it to little more than a legal barrier between the workers and management.

We are responsible for ourselves and not bound by the permission of the group or the Union. We are the Union.

PART FIVE

Okay, remember in the future, Strand workers: this is how it works...

The rich people who own the business lie about what they can afford so that they can turn the screws on you and get even richer.

You refuse to believe their bullshit and choose to withhold your labor...

...thus taking away their profits until their bluff has been called, and they treat you with some respect.

And two years from now, when your lousy postmodern novel has not been published and your band isn't making any money...

I will definitely remind you not to fuck up again.
Thank you.

READ B4 U VOTE
Gimme one hundred dollars and shoot yourself in the foot!
Hmm...

You don't have to do that!
UAW

You're legally protected. I'm stronger than him.

And I brought the crew. We got your back.

Okay, gimme 80 dollars and just punch yourself.
Well, that seems fair...

No! Don't give him anything! Why would you? You only stand to lose!
Well, he keeps asking!

So? We'll stay here and fight them until they get the point!

...WE AIN'T GIVIN' YOU SHIT!

You're right! We can keep fighting! But what if they never leave?
Well, we're going to need to put pressure on them.

Are you talking about a... a strike!?

Maybe, but we're not there yet. First we need to vote to authorize a strike.
But I'll lose wages! I'll be sticking my neck out!

It's not a strike. It's just a vote to authorize a strike. If we wanted to strike, there would be a whole separate vote for that.

In order to strike, we would need the approval and support of our union's international office, a large organization in Detroit.
Probably a lot of bureacracy.

With a strike authorization vote certified by the international, our strike fund would pay 100% of our health insurance premiums and pay us each 200 dollars a week for 40 hours on the picket line.

But it would take a few weeks to get the ball rolling, so a strike authorization vote just tells them to be ready.
Just in case.

There's no risk, it doesn't cost you anything, and it sends a clear message to management to
stop messing around!

If the company sees that you are serious, and united as a workforce, they won't risk a strike.
They have too much to lose.

Even still, an effective strike could get you back pay and benefits, much more valuable in the long run.
The company could lose thousands.

VOTE "YES"

to authorize a strike.

I grew up on a farm so, though the next few statements seem absurd, they are true.

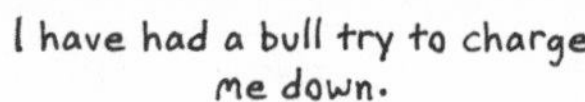
I have had a bull try to charge me down.

I have seen a fire consume my great-grandfather's three-story barn.

While trying to herd calves off a frozen pond, I've had the ice crack under me.

Every time I sit down at negotiations with the store, I think about how I would rather face all of those things again and at the same time than hear that same line repeated:

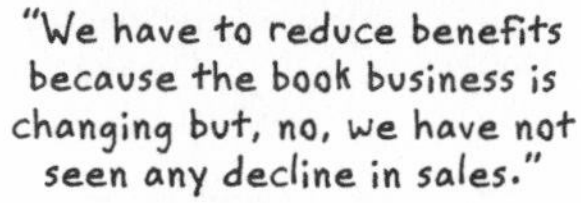
"We have to reduce benefits because the book business is changing but, no, we have not seen any decline in sales."

Regarding negotiations, it's as if they want to give the employees the worst deal possible regardless of the long range results to the store.

Since their side is being conducted by their lawyer, Harry, this is indeed exactly what is happening.

Fred's too old or just doesn't want to be involved. Nancy is leaving everything to Eddie and Harry, which is pathetically irresponsible.

Eddie is following Harry's lead. This is also none too bright, since Harry doesn't work here and can't possibly care about the store the way the workers do.

The Strand used to reward intelligence. We now pander to stupidity.

Hopefully, the day will soon come when the Strand once again upholds the values that make New York the greatest city in the world.

Nancy bass officially joined the Strand team at age 25. She later became part owner.

In May 2012, to commemorate the store's 85th anniversary, ownership threw itself a lavish public party in its rare book room hosted by Bravo network's Andy Cohen...

...the man behind such television hits as *Queer Eye*, *Project Runway*, and the *Real Housewives* franchise.

Adding to the cause for celebration, Nancy Bass Wyden had announced earlier that week that she and her husband, senator Ron Wyden of Oregon, were expecting their third child together.

Senator Wyden has a history of supporting labor and voting in favor of workers' rights.

Last election cycle he received $72,500 from various unions. In 2007, he voted to restrict employer interference in union organizing.

He voted to extend unemployment benefits from 39 weeks to 59 weeks, and is rated 92% by the AFL-CIO, indicating a pro-union voting record.

...with a net worth of at least 15.4 million, Wyden's big gain came after he married Nancy Bass, owner of New York's Famous Strand Bookstore, in 2005

oregonian Sept 1, 2011

Needless to say, he and his family likely enjoy the finest healthcare available.

Among the workers, there was much discussion regarding what action we would take to seize the narrative of the day and most effectively disrupt the party.

Another round of negotiations were scheduled for earlier that day in what appeared to be management's hopes of finally settling our dispute to best avoid any disturbance.

The event's unusually early 5 pm start time, before the end of the first shift, was perceived as an effort to mitigate employee attendance and a sign that the company had considered us in its planning.

Lately, a few of the more radical among us have been discussing the specifics of a sit-in, where a group of workers, on the clock, would gather on the sales floor and sit in protest.

The group would refuse to work until a representative from the union local came to the store to diffuse the situation, the protocol as specified in our contract. The party would provide an ideal opportunity.

I was opposed to this idea. Participation would undoubtedly invite significant repercussions and they would not be uncalled for.

The individuals most devoted to fighting the store would gather of their own volition like lambs to the slaughter, and could be subsequently fired, thereby weakening our base.

Legal precedents were cited wherein a worker's right to sit were upheld in court, but many of those cases were in protest of a specific Unfair Labor Practice or policy...

...as opposed to general dissatisfaction with the state of contract negotiations. We could not reasonably expect the local or the courts to support us.

In an effort to be more hands-on and available to the group, Vilma attended one of our meetings, at which she strongly warned against this type of action.

Moreover, having been made aware of the plan, she would be legally culpable had she not taken measures to prevent it happening on this or any other day. The sit-in was off.

As a safer alternative, the local supported and helped organize another picket to take place outside the store during the event, just three floors down. Staff wore all black.

Some workers voiced an intention to aggressively disrupt the party itself, only to later discover they had been blacklisted by management and were barred from entering.

A number of large, grey-suited men were seen standing authoritatively outside the store since early afternoon, ready to diffuse any serious situation.

The workers were unfazed, picketing outside the store for nearly three hours. Meanwhile, upstairs, ownership sipped champagne with minor celebrities and toasted to their fortune.

Ultimately, our aims were two-fold and in each we were successful: to target management, casting a pall upon their party, and to further increase public awareness of our situation.

While the fever to fight back had been steadily spreading in our ranks, there was significant overlap of those who attended worker meetings and those who joined the picket line…

But still, worker ranks once again swelled with friends, former employees, and a healthy show of support from the general public.

People frequently inquire as to how they can help us. Some offer money, services, meeting places, etc.—all of which we need and appreciate. But, troublingly, others reflexively boycott the store.

While I don't encourage anyone to cross a picket line, a boycott of the store would only legitimize management's claims of financial suffering.

Instead, voice your support of the staff, and buy books. Show ownership that you prefer a store where knowledge and culture are prized over kitschy souvenirs and ephemera…

…and where employees and people are valued over dollars. Continue to support independent businesses, used books, The Strand, and its staff so that they may thrive together for decades to come…and write a letter to a senator!

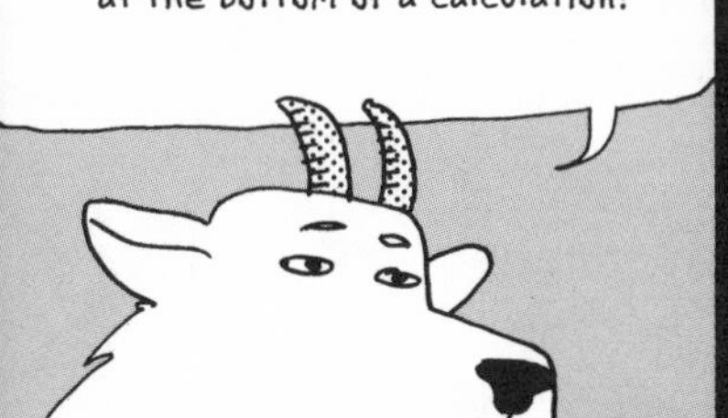
How can an institution that professes to champion free speech and individuality treat its employees as if they are numbers at the bottom of a calculation?

I worked at Strand for close to fifteen years. When I started, the Strand was very much like a family. You could come to management with any problem and a solution would be found.

When they thought they had a reason to fire me, they were so quick to jump at the chance that they put themselves in a position where I could have sued them for unlawful termination.

I did not have the heart to sue Fred, for he had given me a great job for well over a decade. With the union's help, we came to a settlement that both sides could live with.

I know so many great, hardworking people who were fired just so the company could hire someone else and pay them less. They clearly are being penny smart and pound foolish.
Greener pastures

Until Strand management stops trying to break up the union and starts to treat its employees with the respect they deserve, I refuse to patronize the Strand.

Ever since my first election, the 2000 presidential, I've come out on the losing end. Hell, even before that if you count the mascot vote at my brand new elementary school...

...when my friends and I campaigned for pitbull only to lose out to penguin. I'm not sure why I've always been an election loser.

I don't consider myself an extremist, and I don't feel that I've latched onto causes that are far out there. All in all, the idea of voting has left me a little disillusioned.

The thing is, whenever I look back on the sides that have won those elections, I don't see a group of people voting with their hearts for a cause they believe in.

I see people choosing the lesser of two evils. I see people making excuses for keeping the status quo.

When are people going to stop taking this mentality into the voting booth? When are people going to stand up for what's right?

PART SIX

Peace out!

In an effort to better handle negotiations, the UAW national office dispatched June Benjamin to aid our local and negotiating committee at the table.

In shuttle diplomacy, a state-supplied mediator meets with each party to try and draw them out of their obstinacy. This is where compromises are forged. Nothing proposed to the mediator at this time is binding. There have been no agreements.

While ownership has consistently and unbudgingly demanded givebacks, a rumor emerged that the two-tier system was officially withdrawn as a result of these sessions.

But this turned out to not be the case. It seemed possible that the local was withholding information from the stewards or misrepresenting events. None of the workers were clear on the details.

Negotiations had been moving slowly. The Strand ultimately proposed three subtly different, mildly confusing contracts, all of which were stacked against the workers and unacceptable.

All three forced us to choose from a menu of our most collectively valuable givebacks, and make concessions in other areas to offset the cost of that choice to the company.

The main contentions on both sides were personal day/holiday pay, wages, and healthcare. Our official stance in negotiations had been that the terms of our current contract remain unchanged.

Many of us were prepared to accept nothing less. In a final effort to push the store to acquiesce, the local finally planned to authorize a strike.

There was still a lot of confusion among the workers as to whether a vote to authorize a strike would serve as a vote explicitly in favor of going on strike...

...or if there would be a separate, second vote to strike if the new proposal was rejected and our demands still not met.

Pablo implied an imminent strike if we were not satisfied by July 1, 2012, scaring many in our ranks who could not afford to sacrifice any wages. But it seemed the store was equally unnerved...

Within days, the workers had a new, slightly improved offer on the table from ownership. A vote on this proposal would be coupled with our upcoming vote to authorize a strike. A vote for one would be a vote against the other.

Actions were planned in the days preceding the vote. Some of us felt we were just getting started, while others saw a comfortable end coming to the turmoil at their workplace.

I felt optimistic that the workers would reject all previous proposals and continue to fight at no added cost or risk to them or their families.

But on June 14th 2012, the workers of the Strand Bookstore voted to accept the terms of the slightly revised contract put forth by management, thereby imposing upon all current and future employees the terms outlined therein for the duration of three years.

There would be no actions, no strike and no further word on the matter. We had sealed our fate.

It has been just over one year since our bitter defeat. The presence of the Occupy movement has visibly dwindled. Verizon workers spent summer weeks on strike demanding fairer compensation.

In that year, there has been a massive overhaul of Strand personnel, with a focus on pushing out older, more highly paid, long unionized workers...

...and steadily replacing them with recent college graduates in the presumed hopes of more frequent turnover. Paltry, infrequent raises, fewer benefits, and an oppressive atmosphere provide little incentive to stay on board.

Though thankful for what benefits they do have—of course, it could be worse—new hires are dismayed to learn of their second tier status and slow to come to terms with it.

We've since all become friends. Second-tier workers do not seem unsettled by the fact that over half their colleagues voted to reduce their benfits.

Will they join the fight for more in the coming negotiations? Will they fight to keep what they have? To what extent? Will they accept less? Quit? Will they even still be here?

As of this writing, I am just one month shy of my sixth year at the store. I am capable at my job and I try to make others' jobs easier. I am assuredly a valued employee.

But wherein lies my value? And what is the rate of exchange? Experienced, reliable labor comes at a high price, but seemingly more valuable to the company is what they can save by replacing me with someone new at base rates...

...with little obligation to increase these rates and incentivize long-term employment, thus ensuring turnover, lower-quality service and a weaker union. We have nothing to offer but our obedience.

And so many of us give as little as we can get away with, because that is the example set by the store, and the ethical environment we are encouraged to accept.

Shit, man, I'm a Mets fan. I'm used to rough losses. But in spite of all the world's absurdities and horrors, we have to try to grasp at any glimmer of hope and run with it.

You know, "Ya Gotta Believe." We lost this one for ourselves, even those of us who voted the contract down.

This loss hurt because we could have done it if we'd had more faith in our power.

It seems like a lot of people said, "Yeah, of course I'm voting 'No' but I don't think it'll make a difference."
BRAP

That outlook could have changed the whole mood of the store, could have talked people on the fence out of voting No. Or maybe I'm just desperate for answers.

Call me naive, but I really thought the workers would win this one. I'm pissed, but let's move on. Two years from now? That's our year.

Being tier-two is weird.

In one sense, I am in the union and am very specifically disposed to position myself against the company's various awful practices.

Slights from my bosses are bad but very straightforward.

Slights from the union members of tier-one are different.

The tier one-ers need the new people and yet very unequivocally alienated us in the last round of negotiations.

I'm going to give my full support to this union, whether or not all the older members deserve it.

It's reductive, but the tiered system seems intended to divide employees, and create turnover, and ultimately weaken, if not break, the union.

It's something that should be done away with, but clearly a powerful bargaining chip for managment in the upcoming negotiation.

'Cause if the union gets rid of the tiered system, we'll probably have to give up something else.

I don't qualify for health insurance yet, so the worst of tier-two has yet to hit me.

But having only five personal days sucks. You supposedly get them one-per-month, but with only five...
it's not even one every two.

Every month is pretty tight with rent, food, and having a social life.

I burned through most of my personal days when I was sick at the beginning of the year. I feel somewhat valued sometimes, but feel like that is also exceptional when it happens.

I only make eleven dollars an hour. I need to make three dollars more to feel at all comfortable.

I wonder what will happen when Fred is gone...if it will get much worse.

I mean, I feel like I'm a good example of someone they should value. I work hard, but I still felt degraded for like a year.

I work there because I love books and bookstores and the workers. I work there because the work is honest.

But I don't understand how they treat us. It is like a corporation in that way. Or a factory or something.
(DOOK!)

Switching to part time after being a second-tier union employee is strange. I feel I'm treated mostly as though I'm more experienced than a lot of the full time union employees,

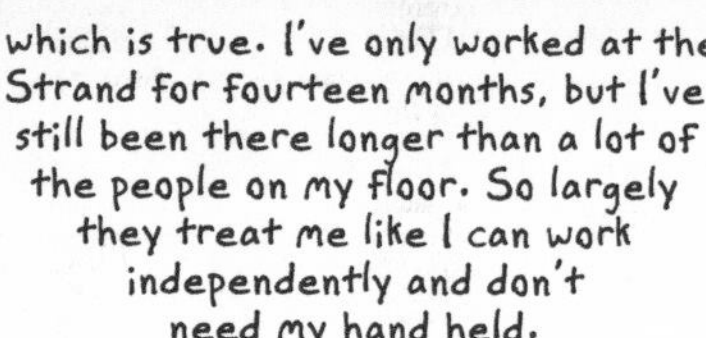
which is true. I've only worked at the Strand for fourteen months, but I've still been there longer than a lot of the people on my floor. So largely they treat me like I can work independently and don't need my hand held.

At times, some of the newer managers have asked me and my coworkers how to do things. The difference for me is that that part time status carries no benefits.
I don't have personal days, nor health insurance, and I don't get paid for holidays. Nothing. It's not so bad because I only work two days a week.

But it is a little unsettling that a new manager can ask me how to perform a task but also has the power to fire me. That's not to say it's all bad, Or that I'm unsatisfied.

Sixteen hours is just enough to where I can stay chummy with my coworkers, who comprise most of my friends in New York, while avoiding the existential crisis that comes with working retail.

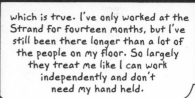

In an apparent effort to combat an "uncomfortable" situation with NYC's homeless population, the Strand had a sprinkler system installed along its copious awning, set to run periodically throughout the night. The red awning was a refuge to groups of vagrants and other homeless individuals who were often too slow to vacate come morning...

...when the Strand work force anchor a fleet of $1-5 clearance book carts along the side of the building.

18 MILES
WE LOVE BOOKS!!

"If you're lying there and you don't know about it, everything is going to get soaking wet- all your personal belongings. You're going to freeze, basically."

I wasn't bothered by the use of the sprinklers, as the targets were invariably drugged-out, indolent, and inconsiderate, adding tension to what was already one of our more unpleasant daily tasks.

Some New Yorkers voiced their support of the store and defended its use of the sprinklers, bemoaning a larger homelessness issue of which this is only a symptom.

Many who work at the Strand exhibit signs of perverse glee whenever the store receives bad press. But what is truly perverse is this type of slippery attitude which we come up against during negotiations, where claims are made which are hard to trust or take seriously.

When asked about the sprinklers:

Strand markets itself as supportive of the community which they credit with having a hand in the store's storied success...

...while literally cleansing themselves of the burden of the community on a nightly basis.

By shortchanging and forcing out their worker base, the Strand contributes to and perpetuates the economic climate which makes it impossible for anyone but the super rich to survive here, leaving one to wonder: who will serve the rich when all the peasants are gone?

Businesses the world over are managed in strict military fashion with little regard for or allowance of personal freedoms, and with little promised in exchange for a worker's time, body, and mind.

Though Strand is perceived by some to be a precious last bastion of old New York authenticity, the associated ideals are sometimes only superficially embraced from within...

...where the business atmosphere is modeled more after that of its corporate rivals. Ironic, in that these models are proving unsustainable, time and again.

I ADVERTISE HERE NY

While there is no reason that a business shouldn't be allowed to evolve its brand and modify its business model (especially after 85 years)...

there is no reason for a thriving company to not provide fair compensation to those who are admittedly in large part at the heart of its self-touted legacy and success.

"New York has Closed Itself off to the young and struggling. New York has been taken away from you.
Patti Smith again.

The UAW continues to face losses in the south, though not to management. In February 2014 , they suffered an historic defeat when workers at a Chatanooga VW plant voted down a UAW affiliation.
53%
47%
NO
YES

Some saw UAW efforts to organize their plant to be inadequate, and criticized their lack of effort to reach out to and inform workers.
I'M not anti - union, I'M anti UAW.
Mike Burton, VW employee

It was a massive blow to the health and continued strength of the UAW. Some see it to mark the end of organized labor in america.
What the UAW is offering, we can already do without them.
We were only given one choice... It's BS.

In December, 2013, UAW considered hiking membership dues by 25 percent, as it faces dwindling membership and rising operating costs.
The mission of the UAW has never been more urgent.
Bob King UAW prez.

De-unionization is toxic to our middle class democracy. The supression of new organization has resulted in the dramatic decline of unionization in the U.S.

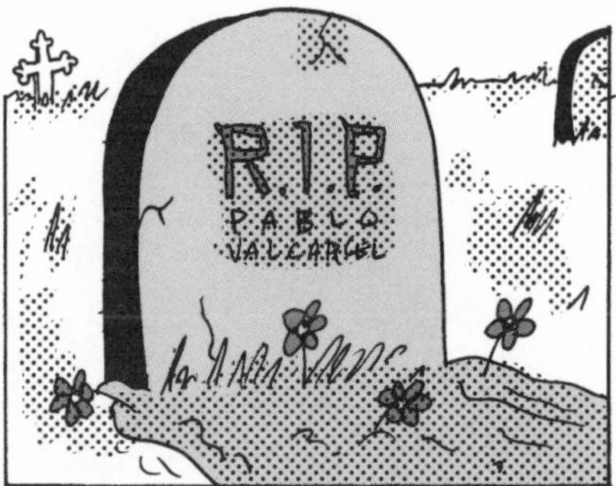
Also in February 2014, our local suffered the loss of President Pablo Valcarcel. His position was succeeded by Vilma Torres-Mulholland. What effect this will have remains to be seen. It could mean new life for our union.
R.I.P.
PABLO VALCARCEL

A recent study defined a low-wage job as one that pays less than $15 an hour; the wage fast food workers demanded in nationwide protests in the summer of 2013.

President Obama advocates a $10.10 national minimum. Bill de Blasio wants $13.00 for NYC. Meanwhile, a NYC living wage is estimated to be 22.66/hr. All are higher than a typical starting wage in NYC.

In the fall of 2014, we will re-enter negotiations with our employer in an effort to define the terms of a new contract in our respective favors.

In the story of the Strand Bookstore, when the legacy of Benjamin Bass and his progeny is rightly celebrated, what will be said of the workers?

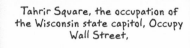

The movements that gave me so much hope last year...

Tahrir Square, the occupation of the Wisconsin state capitol, Occupy Wall Street,

hell, even "Take Back the Strand" feel in jeopardy.

But before they happened, they felt impossible.

Now we know that in this day and age, people will unite to challenge austerity capitalism...
CRASH!

...which means we have to keep fighting. We have no other choice.
THUD

I don't think losing some ground is the same as being defeated.

There are still places where we are continuing the fight.

We're working on starting up the Health and Safety Committee that has always been in the contract but never formed.

Also, we've made a lot of progress towards having workers write evaluations on the performance of their managers.

We keep going, so that we won't be starting from the beginning when we go into the next contract negotiations.

I know it won't be easy, but we can still win. A better workplace is possible.

December, 26. 2013

Strand Bookstore reports the biggest sales day in its 86 year history.

June, 2014

UAW raises dues for the first time in 47 years.

July, 2014

Strand workers reenter negotiations with management.

Solidarity,

G.

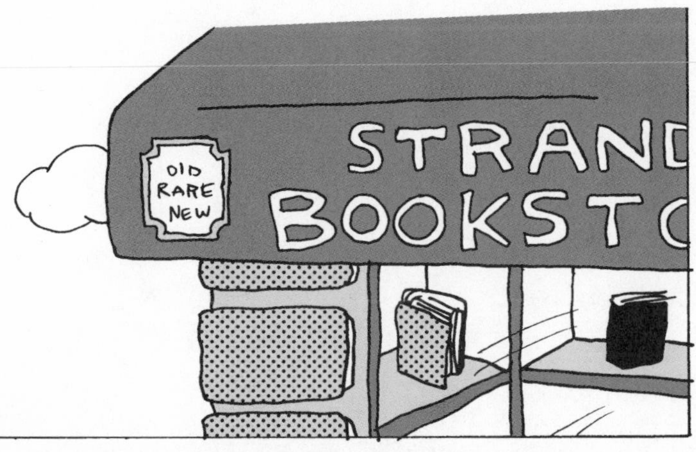

Acknowledgments

The fact that this book exists is a triumph. It would not have been possible without the help and support of Ken Farrell, Gerri Farrell, and my family. One struggle, Larry Lawrence, Sam Calvin, Norhan Hassan, Ashton Walker, Will Bobrowski, Olivia Rosane, Jon Plant, Cyrus Kleege, Maud Pryor, Chris McCallion, Sam Grace Lewis, Joe Morena, all shop stewards, Joe Biel (who had the vision and guts to take on a project like this), Julia Alekseyeva, Paradis, Pie, Bite, Stephanie McMillan, John Farley, Aaron Cometbus, Colin Morse, Alex Cornett, Uzodinma Okehi, all management at the Strand and all UAW Local 2179 associates, Sergio E. Redigolo Gusella, Matt Moses, Grassroots, Meggyn Pomerleau (for her patience during the editing process), and everybody else.
Sorry if I stepped on your toes.

Special thanks to Maud Pryor.
My lover, my letterer...

Protest photo by Sam Calvin
Author photo by Ken Farrell
"Negotiations" by Will Bobrowski

Read *"Stick and Stay, They're Bound to Pay"*
by Ethan Heitner at
graphichistorycollective.com

NOTES:

Page 30: Comments sourced from the internet
Page 35, Panel 1: The event was James Franco promoting *Dangerous Book Four Boys.*
Page 36, Panel 4: Hear my rap music at McBurbs.bandcamp.com
Page 38, Panel 4: Walgreens and Duane Reade are essentially the same company now.
Page 41: The business is called Just Kids Nostalgia
Page 45, Panel 4: The book depicted is *Everything Matters* by Ron Currie Jr.
Page 84, Panel 5: This is the flyer front/back

Page 100, Panel 6: Write Ron Wyden at http://www.wyden.senate.gov/contact/
or
911 NE 11th Ave., Suite 630
Portland, OR, 97232
tel (503) 326-7525

CREDITS:

Maud Pryor
Jon Plant
Cyrus Kleege
Andy Gleeson
Colin Morse
Jesse Dowell
Al Angel
Matt Glasser
J. Atencio
Uzodinma Okehi
Liz Baldwin
Olivia Rosane
Angel
Will Bobrowski
Marta Zemanuell
Patrick Fairnbach
Cristen Jaynes
Michael Chin
Nate Warden

Sources

50 Cent. *Heat.* Dr. Dre, 2003. CD.

"About Strand Strand History at Strand Books." *About Strand.* strandbooks.com/strand-history

"Bass Real Estate LLC." *Manta.* manta.com/c/mm58rcr/bass-real-estate-llc

Berman, Jillian. "$10.10 Minimum Wage Would Actually Create New Jobs: Study." *The Huffington Post,* 19 Dec. 2013. huffingtonpost.com/2013/12/19/1010-minimum-wage_n_4474183.html

Berman, Jillian. "Telling Fast Food Workers To 'Get A Better Job' Is Nonsense, In 1 Chart." *The Huffington Post,* 11 Dec. 2013. huffingtonpost.com/2013/12/11/low-wage-jobs_n_4421095.html?ir=Business

Brooks, Thomas R. *Toil and Trouble; a History of American Labor.* New York: Delacorte, 1971.

Carlson, Erin. "'Star Wars' Creator George Lucas Fires Back at Fanboys, 'Red Tails' Snub." *The Hollywood Reporter.* hollywoodreporter.com/heat-vision/george-lucas-star-wars-red-tails-282905

Cervantes. "Independent Bookstores See Opportunity in Corporate Suffering." *Literary Manhattan.* literarymanhattan.org/independent-bookstores-see-opportunity-in-corporate-suffering/

Croh, Eric. "A Darker Future for "Tier 2" Workers." *Home.* remappingdebate.org/article/darker-future-tier-2-workers

Dray, Philip. *There Is Power in a Union: The Epic Story of Labor in America.* New York: Doubleday, 2010

"Drivetrain Approach to Recommender Systems." *Big Data Now Current Perspectives from O'Reilly Media:* 2012 Edition. Sebastopol, CA: O'Reilly Media, 2012. 26.

Elk, Mike. "After Historic UAW Defeat at Tennessee Volkswagen Plant, Theories Abound." *Working In These Times.* inthesetimes.com/working/entry/16300/after_uaw_defeat_at_volkswagen_in_tennessee_theories_abound

Farley, John. "Picket Line at the Strand and Evolving Labor Tactics." *MetroFocus.* thirteen.org/metrofocus/2012/05/picket-line-at-the-strand-and-evolving-labor-tactics/

Flanagan, Jane. "Family Owners Have Always Been Hands-on at Strand." *The Villager.* thevillager.com/villager_368/familyowners.html

"George Packer: Is Amazon Bad for Books?" *The New Yorker.* Web. newyorker.com/reporting/2014/02/17/140217fa_fact_packer?currentPage=all

Goldensohn, Rosa. "Strand Books Used Sprinklers to Douse Homeless, Employees Say." *DNAinfo New York.* dnainfo.com/new-york/20131114/greenwich-village/strand-books-yanks-warning-signs-for-sprinklers-used-douse-homeless.

Hall, LeeAnn. "Living Wage Job Gap Calls for Charting a New Course for U.S. Economy." *TheHill.* thehill.com/blogs/congress-blog/economy-budget/192654-living-wage-job-gap-calls-for-charting-a-new-course-for-us

Hawkins, Andrew. "Deal Portends $13 Minimum Wage." *Latest from Crains New York Business.* crainsnewyork.com/article/20140602/BLOGS04/140609985/cuomo-deal-portends-13-minimum-wage-for-nyc>.

Heitner, Ethan. "The Flint Sit-Down Strike in Comics." *Dissent Magazine.* Ed. Paul Buhle. 17 Sept. 2012. dissentmagazine.org/online_articles/the-flint-sit-down-strike-in-comics

Hell, Richard. *I Dreamed I Was a Very Clean Tramp: An Autobiography.* New York: Ecco, 2013.

Hobson, Jeremy. "The Bookstore in the Digital Age." *Marketplace.org* marketplace.org/topics/life/bookstore-digital-age

Jeltsen, Melissa. "Verizon Workers On Strike Over Contract." *The Huffington Post.* TheHuffingtonPost.com, 07 Aug. 2011. huffingtonpost.com/2011/08/07/verizon-workers-strike_n_920354.html

Kusisto, Laura. "Is Detroit the New New York? Ask Patti Smith." *New York Observer.* observer.com/2010/09/is-detroit-the-new-new-york-ask-patti-smith/

Mapes, Jeff. "Ron Wyden, Mr. Regular Guy, Now One of Capitol Hill's 50 Richest." *OregonLive.com.* blog.oregonlive.com/mapesonpolitics/2010/09/ron_wyden_mr_regular_guy_now_o.html

"New York History Walks." *New York History Walks.* nyhistorywalks.wordpress.com/tag/strand-books/

Pope, Charles. "Sen. Ron Wyden's Wife Nancy Is Pregnant, Due in December." *OregonLive.com* oregonlive.com/politics/index.ssf/2012/05/sen_ron_wydens_wife_nancy_is_p.html

"Preamble." *36th UAW Constitutional Convention.* Web. uaw.org/page/preamble

"Ron Wyden on Jobs." *On the Issues.* ontheissues.org/domestic/Ron_Wyden_Jobs.htm

Schnapp, John. *The Wall Street Journal.* Dow Jones & Company. online.wsj.com/news/articles/SB10001424052702304675504579391163334785396

Smith, Patti. *Just Kids.* New York: Ecco, 2010.

"Staff Picks." *Strand Books.* strandbooks.com/staff-picks/

"Strand Bookstore." *Wikipedia.* Wikimedia Foundation, 06 Oct. 2014. en.wikipedia.org/wiki/Strand_Bookstore>.

"The Strand Had a Really Good Christmas." *WNYC News.* wnyc.org/story/least-one-bookstore-had-merry-christmas/

Szczesny, Joseph. "UAW Faces Revolt Over Two-Tier Wages." *TheDetroitBureaucom RSS.* thedetroitbureau.com/2011/08/uaw-faces-revolt-over-two-tier-wages/

"Union Facts | United Auto Workers, Local 2179 | Profile, Membership, Leaders, Political Operations, Etc." *Union Facts.*

"United Automobile Workers." *Wikipedia.* Wikimedia Foundation, 06 July 2014. en.wikipedia.org/wiki/United_Automobile_Workers

Warburton, Simon. "COMMENT: Bob King Cites American Dream to Fight UAW Corner." *Just-auto.com.* just-auto.com/comment/bob-king-cites-american-dream-to-fight-uaw-corner_id142035.aspx

White, Jerry. "World Socialist Web Site." *UAW Membership Continues to Plummet* -. wsws.org/en/articles/2010/04/uawm-a01.html>.

Williams, Douglas. "How The UAW Lost Chattanooga." *The South Lawn.* Web. thesouthlawn.wordpress.com/2014/02/17/how-the-uaw-lost-chattanooga/

Writer, Tom Krisher Ap Auto. "UAW Raises Dues for 1st Time in 47 Years." *ABC News.* ABC News Network. abcnews.go.com/Business/wireStory/uaw-raises-dues-1st-time-47-years-23978826

Cartoonist/rapper Greg Farrell was born and raised in Huntington, Long Island. He is the co-editor of *Strandzig*, a Strand worker-sourced arts and literature zine (available upon request). He now lives in Brooklyn, NY, his corresponding metropolis.

DoctorMobogo@gmail.com
@DoctorMobogo
yoburbalino.blogspot.com

SUBSCRIBE TO EVERYTHING WE PUBLISH!

Do you love what Microcosm publishes?

Do you want us to publish more great stuff?

Would you like to receive each new title as it's published?

Subscribe as a BFF to our new titles and we'll mail them all to you as they are released!

$10-30/mo, pay what you can afford. Include your t-shirt size and month/date of birthday for a possible surprise! Subscription begins the month after it is purchased.

microcosmpublishing.com/bff

...AND HELP US GROW YOUR SMALL WORLD!